*The Emotional Hostage*

Other FuturePace Books by the Authors:

**KNOW HOW**
Guided Programs for Inventing Your Own Best Future
(with David Gordon)

**THE EMPRINT METHOD**
A Guide to Reproducing Competence
(with David Gordon)

**SOLUTIONS**
Practical and Effective Antidotes for Sexual and Relationship Problems
(Cameron-Bandler)

# *The Emotional Hostage*

RESCUING YOUR EMOTIONAL LIFE

*Leslie Cameron-Bandler*
*Michael Lebeau*

FuturePace, Inc.
San Rafael, California

Published by
FuturePace, Inc.
P.O. Box 1173
San Rafael, California 94915

ISBN 0-932573-03-7
Library of Congress Catalog Number 85-081627

Text design by Joy Dickinson

Cover design by Bill Fulton

*This book is dedicated*
*with respect and affection to*
*Wally Aron,*
*Jessie Wood,*
*Dan Chabot,*
*Becky Pigott,*
*and Howard ("Nemo") Nemerovski.*

We pass through this world but once. Few tragedies can be more extensive than the stunting of life, few injustices deeper than the denial of an opportunity to strive or even to hope, by a limit imposed from without, but falsely identified as lying within.

STEPHEN JAY GOULD
*The Mismeasure of Man*

# Contents

1

# *The Emotional Hostage*

WE LIVED STORYBOOK LIVES. AT LEAST IT SEEMED THAT WAY to our families, friends, colleagues, and students. As evidence they pointed to our professional success, our lovely home and happy child, and our romantic and passionate love for each other. But behind the trappings of professional success, hidden from those around us, was a life of recurring torment. We were hostage to a powerful but little understood force: our own emotions. In our first attempts to struggle free of the grip of our emotions, we learned to appreciate the seriousness of our plight. We also discovered that we were not alone.

All of us are hostage to our emotions in one way or another.

Some people are confined and constrained by their fear of the intensity of such emotions as inadequacy, sadness, hurt, and rejection. For these people, emotions are like land mines; they tiptoe through life trying to avoid dangerous feelings. At the first hint that a strong emotional response is underfoot, they withdraw. They avoid situations that appear to be emotionally highly charged, such as a heated argument with a loved one, visiting an acquaintance who is suffering from cancer, or spending time with a friend who is depressed. In order to spare themselves the sting of hurt and rejection, they refrain from reaching out to others. They also steer clear of professional challenges. This way they can avoid tripping over unpleasant surprises, such as feelings of inadequacy. As a ransom, these people avoid huge areas of life in the way that some people avoid seeing scary movies. In the process, they are usually successful at keeping themselves from experiencing much of what is worthwhile in life.

Other people can never express their potential because the emotions they experience, such as fear, inadequacy, and doubt, keep them from ever taking action, let alone risk. As hostages to their emotions they are locked in a kind of paralysis. A lonely woman feels shy, so she doesn't interact. An unemployed mother feels inadequate, so she behaves stupidly even though she is a very intelligent woman. A teenager feels afraid of failing or looking foolish, so he doesn't learn new skills such as dancing, speaking in front of a group, or drawing. A middle-aged housewife feels insecure, so she never takes a step outside her familiar domain, even though she feels bored and resentful in it.

Many people are victims of repetitive kidnappings by their emotions. Strong emotions will hit them, like a series of waves, and carry them away from whatever train of thought or activity they were engaged in. These people may finally give up hope of ever reaching their destinations. Others are seduced by the sense of comfort they achieve by clutching onto only a handful of familiar emotions. They blind themselves to the incredible range of color, shading, and nuance in the full palette of emotions that is the birthright of every human being to enjoy. The price they pay for their comfort is a drastically diminished life.

Some people are slaves to other people's emotions. A client of ours was in this predicament. If her husband was confident about closing a business deal, she could feel relieved. As long as her child was happy, she could feel contented. If her best friend felt hopeful about saving her troubled marriage, our client could feel a moment of relaxation. Her ability to experience valued emotions depended totally on the responses of the people around her. Her emotional footing was based on their moods. Each time their moods changed, which of course was often, it was like having the rug pulled out from underneath her. She spent a great deal of her time attempting to put others in a good mood so that she could have a moment of pleasure for herself. She resembled a juggler who was trying to keep fifteen dishes spinning on sticks—all day, every day. Not surprisingly, she described herself as always fighting to keep her balance.

In their efforts to relieve the pain of unpleasant emotions, or to reach a pleasurable state, some people become slaves to drugs. Heroin, cocaine, marijuana, alcohol, sugar, uppers, downers, nicotine, and caffeine are all mood-altering substances. People who rely on them are making an effort to change or to reach emotions by choice. But in the process they become a hostage to the drug. Choice and control are traded for addiction.

There is another kind of price that many of us pay for the unpleasant emotions we endure. It has been clinically proven that people suffer physiological illnesses as a result of chronically enduring such emotions as fear, humiliation, worry, pressure, anger, inadequacy, helplessness, and so on. Over time, such emotions can generate dangerous levels of stress, leading to high blood pressure, ulcers, heart disease, and other degenerative illnesses.

In his book *Is It Worth Dying For?,* Dr. Robert S. Eliot describes the results of his investigations as a cardiovascular consultant seeking to determine why aerospace workers at Cape Canaveral were suffering more, and more severe, heart attacks than would have been expected.

> The problem, I found, was not the firing of rockets but the firing of people. The government had started making the space race a lower national priority, and each time there was a successful launch, 15 percent of the workers who made it happen were fired . . . . Physical and laboratory exams of engineers at the Cape showed no unusual level of the standard coronary risk factors. What I found instead were *anxiety and depression and a universal, pervasive feeling of hopelessness and helplessness.* (emphasis added) [p. 15]

The stress of this constant fear of losing their jobs—and the attendant security and prestige—resulted in a professional population that "led the nation in drinking, drug-taking, divorce, and sudden heart-attack deaths." Dr. Eliot goes on to describe laboratory studies done with many different kinds of animals, all of which demonstrate a direct and significant link between emotional stress and physiological well-being.

> One of the most compelling cases for the adverse effect of long-term stress is what I call the "fourteen-foot risk factor" for heart disease. The Hamadryas baboon forms a strong lifelong attachment to its mate. Russian researchers removed male baboons from their mates and placed them some distance away—perhaps 14 feet—in a separate cage and in full view of the mate. A new male was placed in the female's cage. The displaced baboon was forced to observe his long-term mate with a new lover. He was helpless to change the situation, yet had to endure it. With no alteration in diet or any other factor, within six months the baboons experienced the whole spectrum of heart disease in the modern industrial world: some developed high blood pressure, some had heart attacks, and some died of sudden cardiac death.
>
> Animals are not humans, of course, but it seems very likely that in humans, too, a sense of helplessness and hopelessness can fire off stress chemicals that overpower the body's resistance. That's what happened to the Cape Canaveral aerospace engineers. [pp. 16–17]

There are many ways to be taken hostage, held captive, and harmed by your emotions, but the result is always the same. Emotional hostages spend much of their lives in service to their emotions, or even in sacrificing their lives to their emotions, instead of their emotions being in the service of their lives. As you are about to discover, we—the authors of this book—were held captive, in different ways, by our emotions. Leslie had little choice over which emotions she experienced from moment to moment, wasn't able to predict what was coming next, and thus had no ability to protect herself from the onslaught. She lived in an emotional reality that was as intense as it was dictatorial. Michael's fear of unpleasant emotions led him to develop a blustery and forceful persona, but otherwise kept him tentative and introverted. When he did experience the sting of hurt, anger, or rejection, he was caught in an intensifying downward spiral that maintained its painful grip for weeks, or even months. This left him feeling desperate, dependent, and victimized.

This book is the story of the actions we took, after years of unwittingly paying a ransom, to free ourselves from being hostage to the demands and vagaries of our emotions. The journey begins with an awareness of how emotions can hold us in the service of outcomes that are contrary to our well-being, proceeds to a new realm of understanding about how and why emotions are generated, moves to a level of personal competence in selecting, expressing, and using emotions, and ends with a vision of a future in which everyone experiences the freedom and power of emotional choice.

Our purpose in writing this book is to start you out on the road to that future, by helping you learn how to rescue your own emotional life. In the following pages we celebrate the value and pleasure inherent in emotions, and we also point out the toll that can be exacted by inappropriate unchecked emotions. Each chapter contains tips, guidelines, and techniques you can use to make an immediate difference in your life. By the time you finish reading the final chapter of this book, you will know how to break whatever emotional bonds exist in your life. Whether or not you actually free yourself is up to you. We can point you in the right direction and give you all the maps, instructions, and gear you need to home in on your destination. But knowing that you *can* gain freedom and power by attaining emotional choice isn't the same as *having* emotional choice. It is up to you to gather up those supplies and put right foot in front of left. When you do, you will no longer be a tool of your emotions. Instead, you will have the tools you need to put your emotions in the service of your personal and professional goals.

But before we lead you on your journey, let us tell you more about what happened on ours. (In Chapter 3 we'll explain at greater length what we mean by the term "emotions." For now, as we tell you more about ourselves and as we introduce some of the concepts we'll be working with throughout this book, the working definition of "emotions" is *your overall subjective experience at any given moment.*)

## *The Rescue of an Emotional Hostage: Michael Introduces Leslie*

In 1982, at the age of thirty-two, Leslie was a successful researcher, therapist, teacher, and author. Her area of study was human communication and change. The techniques she helped develop for enhancing communication styles and accomplishing personal change had been adopted by tens of thousands of psychologists and counselors. She was instrumental in establishing an international network of training institutes. Her books were used to train therapists, and they were making a significant difference in the ability of those therapists to achieve results with their clients. Educators and businesspeople were beginning to show an interest in learning how to apply her methodology to their endeavors, and as a result of her work thousands of people each year were enjoying the exhilarating effects of personal transformation. Whether through her work or through personal relationships, people enjoyed the benefits of Leslie's intelligence, caring, and compassion.

She was surrounded with the trappings of professional fulfillment. She was admired and respected not only for her work, but also for how she breathed life into it by exemplifying its principles in her interactions with others. Many of her students, friends, and colleagues used her as a role model. But she knew something about herself that they didn't: her emotional life was a maelstrom.

Most people experience at least a handful of different emotions each day. Some people go through a dozen or more emotional changes in a day. But Leslie would sometimes be buffeted by a dozen such changes in an hour's time. And for every change in emotion there was a corresponding change in her behavior. This resulted at times in inconsistent responses to the same circumstances. For instance, whenever she discovered that our thirteen-year-old son, Mark, had failed to do something he was supposed to do—a common occurrence with most thirteen year olds—her response would vary depending on how she was feeling at the moment. If she was feeling harried after a long, tough day, she might unleash a furious verbal assault on his irresponsible and inconsiderate behavior—only to apologize minutes later. If she happened to be feeling generous, she would be understanding, sympathetic to his plight, make excuses for him, and then end up doing "it" for him.

At work she would respond to similar requests and events at different times as either inconveniences, opportunities, crises, obligations, or impositions, depending on whether at the moment of hearing the news she was feeling concerned, ambitious, anxious, responsible, or discouraged. Her assistants found it difficult to formulate policy or to prepare adequately, because they never knew which opinion would be prevailing that day, or hour. And Mark wasn't learning the connection between present actions and future consequences that we wanted him to have. How could he, in the face of his mother's mixed and contradictory responses? In almost all areas of her life her rapidly changing emotions, not the outcomes that she desired, controlled her responses.

On the bright side, there was never a dull moment when you were with Leslie. It's true that settling into marriage with her was a little like settling down to a meal in the front row seat of a roller coaster. But I always knew that, just as with the mercurial meteorological manifestations in the Rockies, if I didn't like the current emotional weather all I had to do was wait a short while and it would change.

One aspect of Leslie's emotional life *was* consistent, though. Regardless of the situation, regardless of the emotion she was experiencing, regardless of the emotion that would have been the most appropriate guide to behavior in the situation, what she wanted to feel, and what she was always trying to feel, was "worthwhile." Unfortunately, her ability to feel worthwhile depended largely upon her ability to make those around her feel happy and fulfilled—whether or not that was appropriate and useful. And of course it often wasn't. If an assistant made a mistake, Leslie was compelled to try to make him feel good—when secure, curious, responsible, and determined might have been more appropriate for evaluating and correcting the mistake and preventing similar problems in the future. When seminar participants, friends, or colleagues asked for something, Leslie would give it to them if at all possible, whether or not it made sense with regard to her preferences or pre-established outcomes. If they wanted it, and she could give it, they would be happy; then she could feel worthwhile. If Mark wasn't happy about doing his chores, she would spend hours manipulating the situation so that he would feel happy about doing his work, instead of getting him to feel responsible or committed or resigned. If she wasn't successful, she would resolve her frustration by releasing Mark from his obligations and sending him off to play. This solution made him happy; he got what he wanted. It also made her feel good, at least until the next time. In the meantime, Mark quickly became skilled at warding off feelings of happiness in connection with work.

Leslie's compulsion to tend to and nurture the state of happiness in everyone around her—and the talent she developed to do so—served her well as a therapist, set a definite theme for her seminar presentations, and was a tremendous asset in social interactions. But in other situations, such as business meetings, where other criteria are often more relevant to the task at hand, it engendered wasted tangents and a loss of productivity. A greater loss, however, was a string of failed relationships. Leslie's sole concern when hiring and dealing with employees, as well as when choosing and interacting with friends, was "Can I make them happy?" If she could, then all was right with the world. If she couldn't, she felt like a failure. Failure quickly led to feelings of hopelessness, an intolerable state for her. Of course, Leslie taught others to expect her to bring them happiness, as well as most anything else they requested. When this expectation was plowed over with the sharp blade of disappointment and seeded with her sense of failure, irresolvable conflicts grew like weeds. These conflicts stunted, and even destroyed, many of her relationships. It was inevitable. People aren't always happy. Nor should they be required to be.

Like all emotional hostages, Leslie was trapped in patterns of behavior that were dictated by her emotions. It is testimony to her talent, energy, and commitment that, even with the price she was paying in terms of effectiveness, she was able to accomplish all that she had. And she might have continued through life unchanged had conflicts between us over our friends, employees, business dealings, and the parenting of Mark not reached a flash point. Time and accumulating irritations had taken their toll, and the fallout from her responses had become intolerable to me. Her actions often violated my standards for being responsible, and they created constant confusion and disorder in our life—havoc that was often left to me to clean up or repair. My patience and resolve were being eroded by the unrelenting, always changing emotional winds. If the situation didn't change, our marriage would be in jeopardy—and we both knew it.

Fortunately, our expertise is in uncovering patterns and creating effective methods for accomplishing personal change. Once we realized the influence emotions were exerting in Leslie's experience (and mine also, as you will soon discover), we set ourselves the task of researching emotions and developing an effective set of guidelines and techniques for taking control of our emotional lives. We succeeded at that task, but not before discovering that emotions are among the least understood aspects of human experience.

For example, most people believe that emotions lie outside of their control; an emotion is like a pushy houseguest who shows up uninvited, takes over the house, and can't be ignored. An emotion is something to endure or to enjoy, depending on what nature and circumstances will. The same people for whom emotions fall outside the realm of choice *will* choose how to *behave*, however, and then struggle with varying degrees of success to carry out those behaviors. But because they have not had the opportunity to learn how, they will not choose how to feel. Yet, as we will demonstrate in the following chapters, behavior is a *byproduct* of emotions. The easiest and most effective way to guarantee that you will carry out chosen behaviors—from saying "thank you," to selecting a low-calorie meal, to pausing to thoroughly evaluate an objection before responding in a negotiation—is to have selected and accessed the appropriate emotion. Feeling grateful or appreciative *naturally* leads to a heartfelt "Thanks." Feeling determined to become fit *naturally* leads to selecting and eating healthy foods. If you are feeling a combination of curiosity, patience, and concern about overlooking an opportunity, you are going to pause to evaluate at *each* step of the negotiation.

As we demonstrate in Chapters 6, 7, and 8, an important part of achieving emotional choice is knowing how to select and access the most advantageous emotion, when you want and need it. Methods for proper selection and reliable accessing of emotions are two of the requisites for emotional choice that we discovered and eventually formatted into the step-by-step procedures presented in this book.

Once we had developed a comprehensive method for achieving emotional choice, a remedy for emotional servitude, we prescribed a healthy dose for ourselves. Remember Leslie's emotion-limiting patterns of behavior? All that is very different now.

Leslie feels her emotions as intensely and passionately as before, but now she experiences them when she wants them and in a way that supports her well-being. Because her emotional responses no longer distract or dictate, she is able to set outcomes first, then determine how she needs to feel to most effectively accomplish her goals. She looks at new situations in light of her outcomes now, rather than responding from a transient emotion, to evaluate whether to respond to new situations as opportunities, crises, obligations, and so on. This results in more realistic appraisals, a keener judgment, a consistent direction and movement toward her goals, and much less stress for everyone involved.

Because she thinks in terms of the emotions needed to best accomplish each type of goal, for herself and for others, she is no longer compelled to press colleagues or employees (or Mark either) into feeling only happy or fulfilled. Instead, she uses the new techniques she has learned to get them to feel committed, personally significant as a contributor to the project at hand, responsible for completion of agreed upon duties, and, when appropriate, also happy and fulfilled. She now comprehends and appreciates the value, to herself and others, of emotions outside the range of happy and good. Such emotions as frustration, disappointment, and apprehension, for instance, reveal important information and tell her how to best respond to the needs they signal.

Leslie has learned how to move from disappointment to acceptance, and then either to go on to set and pursue new goals, or to try a new approach for resurrecting the fallen expectation. Frustration is now understood as a signal that what she is doing is not working—so if she still wants to accomplish what she was working on she knows she needs to either gather more information, get new instructions, or try a different approach. Frustration can now be easily transformed into patience, helping her to get what is worth going after.

One of the most significant things she learned is how to adjust her perceptions of the past, present, and future to maintain a better relationship between emotions, outcomes, and behavior. For instance, in her former days as a hostage, Leslie might have agreed in February to lead an out-of-state training the following September. When it came time to actually give the training, however, the emotion that influenced her to agree in February was no longer there. So she would find herself away from home, in front of an audience of expectant strangers, acting out of her most recent emotional response—one that often had little or nothing to do with the situation in which she found herself. Naturally, she would regret having accepted in the first place, and would feel disappointed that she had once again gotten herself into such a situation.

But now when Leslie arrives to lead a training, she reviews the values and considerations that were used to make the decision in the past, and she sees through the present into a future in which the benefits of doing this work have *already* been realized. In this way she remembers why she is doing the training, and she gets to feel a positive kind of "responsible" as she sees how her efforts are going to contribute to the attainment of even larger goals in the future. Now when she wants to motivate herself, she looks at exactly how she will help bring a goal into fruition in the future. The result is that she feels determined to accomplish that goal, and confident that she will succeed.

In another and more personal area of her life, Leslie recently became discouraged because she was prevented from participating in a number of activities that were important to her due to a knee injury. Rather than remain discouraged, she set a future goal of being able to run a four-mile trail around a nearby lake. She imagined being able to run the entire distance comfortably and freely, enjoying the exhilarating feeling of this pleasurable movement. She then plotted a course of action that included visits to the doctor, physical therapy, exercise, and even weight training—all of the things that would eventually lead to the accomplishment of her goal. Each action Leslie takes serves to encourage her, increasing her confidence in her ability to reach this goal, even though its full attainment is still months away.

One of the benefits of gaining emotional choice is that it permits you to experience emotions that previously had been denied to you. In Leslie's case, feelings of contentment, acceptance, and patience were mysterious strangers. They were just descriptive words devoid of any actual experience. Before, if she didn't immediately obtain a result she desired, she felt an urgent determination. She was driven and obsessed to make it come out right, right now. As soon as she did accomplish a goal, her attention locked onto the next in line. This is not the recipe for acceptance, patience, and contentment. However, now she can shift her attention to the future, and feel patient, as she sees how she will be working to obtain her desired result over a period of weeks, months, or even years. Extending time lines for action or resolution into the future allows her to accept the fact that not every situation need be resolved in the present. It also makes it possible for her to accept that the people she most cares for will experience unpleasant emotions, and, for the sake of their *future* well-being, that often it is appropriate and necessary that they do.

Using the methods and techniques presented in the following

chapters, Leslie has achieved a degree of choice in her life that she never dreamed would be possible. She has transformed her emotions into tools for living, loving, and expressing life to its fullest. This change is accompanied by new feelings of freedom and safety. When she wakes up in the morning she knows that regardless of the roadblocks, challenges, or inconveniences the day throws at her, she has the means to meet those challenges and sidestep those roadblocks. Her new knowledge and broad range of responses don't prevent her from ever feeling the pangs of such emotions as frustration, disappointment, doubt, and anger, but they do assure that she won't get trapped. She has the choice to learn from them and then move on to more productive or fulfilling emotions. In her words, "Walking through a stretch of sand will slow you down, but that isn't the same thing as being up to your hips in quicksand."

## *The Freeing of Another Hostage: Leslie Introduces Michael*

Michael is a researcher and writer in the field of human behavior, and also a successful businessman and investor. With his astute ability for detecting opportunities, uncanny sense of timing, and finely honed negotiation skills, in less than ten years he parlayed an interest in a single piece of real estate into a small empire of land and commercial and industrial buildings. By the time he was thirty he had made millions of dollars for himself and his fellow investors.

In 1982 Michael was thirty-four, and my husband and colleague. We were breaking new ground with our research, and were collaborating on two books. Due primarily to his efforts, much of our research had been converted into training manuals, videotapes, and workshops. He launched those products in the marketplace and started a publishing company to distribute and market our books. He was not only the hardest worker I had ever met, he was also the smartest. Everyone who knew him was confident that whatever he decided to do, he would do it well.

But the private Michael had yearnings that no amount of professional success could satisfy. Before I met him, his deepest yearnings—to feel connected, desired, desirable, and loved—had always gone unfulfilled. The mastery that allowed him to sprint to success in other areas of his life failed him in his personal relationships because of the stumbling blocks put in his path by his emotions. Or, to be more accurate, by his lack of knowledge about how to discern and express the few emotions he did experience. A contrast will help you understand his dilemma.

If you ask a friend how she is feeling, she might respond that she feels intrigued, awed, fascinated, curious, appreciative, grateful, encouraged, hopeful, excited, joyful, motivated, determined, enthusiastic, happy, ecstatic, naughty, or carefree. When your friend is feeling good she obviously makes many distinctions about the *kind* of good feeling she is enjoying.

She might also make distinctions among different kinds of unpleasant feelings. Instead of feeling "bad," she feels bored, lonely, lethargic, restless, skeptical, suspicious, sorry, anxious, fearful, nervous, hopeless, irritated, frustrated, disappointed, or insecure. One of the advantages of making such distinctions, rather than being aware only that she is feeling good or feeling bad, is that her emotions indicate what she needs to do to feel something more satisfying. For instance, if she were aware only that she feels bad when visiting relatives, she is left with the option of either not visiting them, or visiting them and enduring the bad feelings. However, if she is aware that she is feeling, say, bored, she not only has the choice of staying away or going and enduring, she also has the choice of doing something to make the visit more interesting. Whenever she knows she is feeling bored, she can search for something that will pique her interest. If she is feeling insecure, she can ask you for reassurance about her place in your life and heart. If she is feeling irritated with you, she can request that you stop your offensive behavior.

But what if your friend had never learned to make those kinds of distinctions? What if she were as naive about the subtleties of emotions as some people are about the subtleties of music, literature, or food? Some people read lines of words in a book with an awareness of metrical pattern, assonance, catalexis, alliteration, and symbolism. Others are aware only that they are reading a poem. Some people have trained their ear to the differences between a rondo, scherzo, sonata, concerto, round, and fugue. To others they are all the same: classical music. Suppose that whenever your friend experienced any kind of unpleasant emotion, all she was aware of was that she was feeling "bad." How would she know what to do or what to ask for so that she could feel good?

What does the feeling "bad" tell you? Other than the obvious—that you're feeling bad—it doesn't tell you much.

Michael was trapped inside such a good/bad world. Life was either bad or good, black or white—but mostly it felt bad. The limited number of emotions he did experience were weighted toward the unpleasant. His repertoire consisted of happiness, loving, and anticipation on one hand, and sadness, hurt, envy, inadequacy, deprivation, insecurity, anger, and resentment on the other. To make matters worse, he was often unaware of his feelings when he was feeling good, but aware of little else other than his feelings when he was feeling bad.

If his friends and family provided him with what he needed at a particular moment, he felt good. If they didn't, he felt bad. But since he rarely knew how to express what he was feeling, getting what he needed was a matter of happenstance. In the few instances in which he did know what he was feeling—hurt or angry, for instance—he lacked useful ways to express those feelings. His reaction usually was to withdraw from those around him, which only served to frustrate them, and to place him more firmly in the painful clutches of the emotion and farther from the reach of those who could have helped him if only he had known how to give them the chance. With no way out, he would remain trapped in a painful emotion for days, or even weeks, without respite. His ordeal would end only when he received, again by chance, what was needed to satisfy the demands of that emotion.

Michael *did* have one reliable way to generate positive feelings. He would fantasize a life in which others responded to him exactly the way he needed in order to satisfy his yearning to feel connected, loved, desired, and desirable. This worked well as long as he could keep the daydream alive. But since he never actually expressed those needs or did anything to specifically elicit those responses, each return to reality was disappointing and disheartening. That is, until we fell in love and married.

I loved him fully and with abandon. My desire for him and bonding to him, together with my sensitivity to the emotional states of others and my dogged determination to make the people around me feel happy and fulfilled (which otherwise was a problem, as you have already seen), made me the perfect antidote for Michael's lack of fulfillment. I wouldn't allow him to withdraw from me. At the first indication that he was feeling bad I would pursue him, literally from room to room if necessary, and I wouldn't stop altering my questions and responses to him until I was sure I had applied the right salve to his wounds. I quickly became facile at recognizing his moods and needs, even when he wasn't sure what they were until I pointed them out. I made sure that he always knew he was loved, desired, and desirable. As our love blossomed, the connection between us grew stronger and more profound. For the first time in as long as he could remember, Michael's deepest yearnings were fulfilled. But one thing remained unchanged. He was still a hostage.

It's true that a complete lack of control had been supplanted with an effective means of dealing with the demands of his emotions. But that "means" depended exclusively on me—it *was* me. We both realized that Michael would not have true emotional choice until he learned how to identify the specific emotion he was experiencing at any given moment, expand the range of emotions he could experience, develop the ability to move out of debilitating ones on his own initiative, and adopt satisfactory ways of expressing all of his emotions. He began work immediately, using our newly developed tools to fashion each one of his new capabilities.

The changes he made over the next few months produced several wonderful, and some unexpected, benefits. His new awareness of emotions, and how to nurture the role they play in engaging and sustaining behavior, makes him more effective than ever as a team-builder, manager, and leader. In affairs of business, he now regularly surpasses his previously established standards and expectations. In affairs of the heart, his ability to know when he is feeling amorous as opposed to needy, for example, or tender as opposed to wanting to belong, makes him more confident and forthright in expressing his needs and desires. He is more sensitive to changes in my emotional landscape, thus more able to respond quickly and appropriately to my needs and desires. The result is that he is more thoughtful, tender, passionate, and compassionate.

A kaleidoscope of new feelings and experiences is now available for him to enjoy. His palette now includes dozens of emotions, ranging from humility and gratitude at one end of the spectrum, to joy and naughtiness at the other. Instead of a life of wandering through a museum viewing the portraits of emotions that others enjoy, he paints his own canvases, choosing and creating emotional experiences such as playfulness, passion, and security, or any others he wants to have, when he wants to have them.

Michael no longer fears certain emotions. He knows how to extract the value hidden in unpleasant and painful emotions and then proceed, using their signals as a springboard to deeper satisfaction. Instead of emotions determining his response and holding sway over his actions, he now evaluates his emotions to determine the best response. This allows him to be the kind of person he most wants to be—sensitive, supportive, and powerful—for himself and for others.

His new ability to choose the best way to express his feelings creates new opportunities for him to get what he wants. For instance, he has learned to orchestrate events that provide him with the emotions he desires. Michael enjoys feeling connected and loved, as well as loving, and finds it especially fulfilling to experience these emotions with regard to young children. He now plans activities with our friends' young children, such as teaching them to ski or sail, or enjoys their companionship for an afternoon at the movies or the zoo. During these times, Michael develops a bond with each child that establishes the basis for a lifelong friendship—as well as feelings of connection and love—that is meaningful to both of them. On a personal level, Michael now makes good things happen in life, not only in fantasy.

## *How Does This Apply to Your Life?*

Even if you have considered the possibility before now, finding your way to a world of emotional choice may seem as daunting as mounting an expedition to a distant star. The direction to move, or even the correct first step, is often unclear. Many people feel less like travelers who are securely progressing along their chosen route than like emotional lightning rods, subject to alternating cycles of calm and fury, as if they were at the center of a storm. Their feelings seem to appear suddenly, washing over them and flooding them with sensations that shape and color their view of themselves and the world around them.

Dr. Robert E. Ornstein, Stanford researcher, author of *The Psychology of Consciousness* and co-author of *The Amazing Brain,* says "Emotions, whether positive or negative, seem to stimulate very strong actions; and it's that signal that makes them so important in our lives. They also help organize experience. They tend to color perception of ourselves and others. Emotions both guide and goad our actions."*

Unfortunately, the problem isn't that most people lack a desirable *degree* of understanding or control over these instigators of behavior—most of the time they lack any worthwhile insight or choice at all.

Many emotions seem to be unpredictable, like the weather, appearing without warning or apparent cause. Pleasant emotions surprise and delight, but too often they are elusive and fleeting. Perhaps you endure unpleasant emotions until you can struggle free of the pressure of their weight and darkness—or until they release you from their grip by going . . . well, the truth is that most of the time you really don't know where they go. You are just thankful for the relief.

Unfortunately, after years of trying different remedies (or the same remedy over and over) without success, frustration turns into disappointment, which in turn leads to discouragement. Sometimes people despair of ever finding relief from the negative control of their emotions, which seem to drain them of power and set the limits for their potential. But that doesn't have to be the case. Your emotions can be the source of change, innovation, and fulfillment. You can learn how to understand the language of your emotions, and how they are signaling the way to the desirable world that awaits you.

Most people don't know it is possible, or even desirable, to appreciate and enjoy all of their emotions. Even fewer realize that the key to emotional choice—the key to learning from and using emotions to achieve life goals—lies within the emotions themselves. Each emotion is a slightly different riddle that has embedded within it the clues you need to benefit from it. But because the clues are not in a form you have been taught to recognize, you may have been missing them—even though you have been looking at them and touching them your entire life.

We have done most of the detective work for you. We have identified the clues and formulated solutions to most of the important riddles. The keys to attaining emotional choice are contained in the following pages in the form of easy-to-understand and easy-to-use techniques.

* From the audiotape, "The Feeling Brain: Emotions and Health."

In the next two chapters we tell you exactly what we mean by emotional choice, and what you can expect to gain from using the techniques introduced in subsequent chapters. In Chapters 4 and 5 we unravel the mystery of the clues we used to solve each emotion's riddle. Chapters 6 and 7 tell you what each emotion is good for—and what it's not good for—and how to know which emotion would be most helpful to you in any particular situation. The answers may surprise you.

Chapter 8 contains four different methods for gaining access to the emotions you want to have, when you want to have them. In Chapter 9 we teach you how to choose a number of ways that are appropriate for you to express each of your emotions, as well as how to know ahead of time the results you can expect when you use each choice.

In Chapter 10 we present a tool called the "Generative Chain." You can use it to extract the valuable learnings from unpleasant emotions, while preventing yourself from becoming trapped in unpleasant feelings. And you can use the methods discussed in Chapter 11 to protect yourself from the punishment that can be imposed by a handful of particularly oppressive emotions.

We intend for this book to give you everything you need—the desire, insight, and know-how—to create for yourself a world of full emotional choice. It's only fair then that in the next chapter we explore just what kind of world that will be by taking a closer peek.

## 2

# *A World of Emotional Choice*

IMAGINE FOR A MOMENT THAT YOU LIVE IN A WORLD IN which you have available to you the full range of human emotions, as well as choices about which of those emotions to experience and how to express them at any given moment. In this world you have access to the sobering unpleasantness of disappointment, anger, and frustration, as well as the exaltation of pride, confidence, and joy. You might wince under the pangs of jealousy, regret, fear, grief, and hopelessness, but only for as long as it takes to extract whatever information these wounds might hold for you. Then you quickly heal and move on. In this world you do not need to mask the feelings that are the expressions of yourself just because you do not know how to satisfyingly express them. Instead, you have access to all of the emotions and behaviors that are the authentic manifestation of who you are and who you want to be. The standard for interactions in this world is a mutually fulfilling dance of emotions and behavior, while stepping on the emotional toes of those around you is a rare mistake.

How close are most of us to living in such a world? What would such a world really be like? As it is now, it's not uncommon for a person who is facing a job interview or sales presentation to feel anxious, his palms breaking out in sweat. He may squirm around, his voice cracking and his attention and concentration ricocheting from one worry to another. No matter how worthy a potential employee he is or how substantive his sales pitch, his presentation will be sabotaged by his anxious feelings, behavior, and appearance. In a world in which emotional choice is a skill that all enjoy, however, this person could choose to present himself with a deep feeling of personal confidence and competence, manifested in his calm demeanor and alert and attentive responses.

Personal lives would be significantly different as well. We all know couples who, as a result of the years of emotional deprivation they have experienced together, seize the opportunity of social situations to sling snide put-downs at one another. Even cloaked as humor, as they often are, such barbs bite deeply, continually adding to the resentment that already scars their relationship. But in a world of emotional choice, it would be difficult to build resentment. Instead, these two people would recognize and respond to their own emotional needs and wants, as well as those of their mate. Over the years, they would experience an increasing sense of trust and security because each day they would have fresh examples of their ability to notice and respond well to the fluctuations of emotional atmosphere that naturally accompany the weather of relationships.

The education each of us receives about our own feelings would also be quite different. Most of us grew up missing out on certain emotional experiences, and wishing we had missed out on others. And yet we need those emotions to which we have no access, and at the same time we seem unable to avoid having access to those we dread. We were taught that there are certain emotions we should not feel, or that we should not express. Yet we *do* feel them, and long to express them—if only it were all right, and if only we knew how. What little education we received about how to recognize the emotional states of those around us was implicit and haphazard at best, and usually aimed at noticing when we had trespassed on dangerous ground. For us, now grown and picking up the pieces, it is time for education and reeducation about the nuts and bolts—and the possibilities—of our emotional lives. This reeducation takes some work; but, like all good work, it is exciting, surprising, interesting, and rewarding.

It is not farfetched to believe that children will someday grow up in a society in which they are taught to take advantage of the full emotional range and choice, as well as the ability to respectfully influence the emotions of others. Leslie and I wrote this book to share our knowledge and tools, believing that once you know what is possible you will reach for those tools, making your own life more nearly what you want it to be. Beyond that, we expect that what you will learn here will be passed on to those whose lives intersect yours, weaving its way through society and through time, forming a seine that will eventually net for our children a future in which the tools presented in this book are taken for granted, and the fulfillment of the emotional life of each individual is ensured.

During our many years of training therapists, as well as working directly with clients and ourselves, we have helped transform a myriad of woes and shortcomings into gratifying personal triumphs—including our own. In every case, the people we were assisting faced essentially the same predicament: They experienced having no choice but to be the way they were in a certain situation. They knew that there were other ways to be, but they just could not seem to make those other possibilities a reality for themselves. As much as they hungered for change, they invariably fell back upon the same old responses to which they were so accustomed.

Are these people revealing an inherent gap in their genetic endowment when they find themselves unable to respond the way they would like? We don't think so. Instead, what is being revealed is that they presently do not know *how* to get themselves to be different—just as tying your shoes was an impossible task until someone who knew how showed you the necessary steps. The justifications for our "failings" and "shortcomings" typically take the form of, "But I was nervous," or afraid, or angry, or jealous, or confused. These are emotions, and what we are revealing when we use them in this way is that something that we are feeling is *holding us in place*—and not the place we want to be.

If you were to sit someone down and ask them what they *really* want for themselves, you would find them naming such emotions as happiness, patience, hope, perseverance, confidence—emotions that seem unattainable, at least in many situations. Certainly, many people would also like to be able to ski, or to be prompt, or to find a better job. But, as we will see, even the attainment of goals like these often depends on emotional change—for example, overcoming *fear* in order to learn to ski, feeling *responsible* to motivate promptness, and feeling *confident* as a catalyst to finding a better job.

So sometimes your emotions are not what you would like to be experiencing in a certain situation. At other times your behavior is largely the *result* of your emotions, so being able to influence your emotions can have wonderful consequences for your ability to change how you interact with the world. If neither of those reasons is sufficient to encourage you to learn to have a choice about your emotions, recall the Cape Canaveral workers and consider the warning that was sounded in the first chapter about the likelihood of suffering an incapacitating illness, or even death, as a result of chronically enduring such emotions as anxiety, fear, helplessness, worry, humiliation, pressure, and inadequacy.

In his books and lectures, Dr. Robert Ornstein discusses recent studies linking emotions and health. For instance, he mentions the case of Norman Cousins, the long-time editor of *Saturday Review,* who describes in his book *Anatomy of an Illness* his treatment for what was thought to be an incurable disease. After his doctors gave up, he gave up on his doctors. He moved himself into a hotel room and prescribed for himself massive doses of humor, starting with the Marx Brothers and Laurel and Hardy. He recovered. Dr. Ornstein admits that one case doesn't constitute a scientific proof, but then goes on to cite scientific studies that *do* demonstrate that your health is linked to the release or expression of your emotions.

> While there is some anecdotal evidence for laughter, single cases do not provide adequate scientific evidence. However, there is one area of research on cancer where the link between emotional expression and health is supported by many studies. A large num-

> ber of studies has found that a characteristic of lung cancer patients is that they suppress their emotions. Cancer patients seem to ignore their negative feelings such as hostility, depression, and guilt. A recent study that compared long-term survivors of breast cancer with those who do not survive found the same pattern. The long-term survivors express, to themselves and to many other people, much higher levels of anxiety, hostility, alienation, and other negative emotions than short-term survivors. They have more negative moods, they express more negative attitudes towards their illness and towards almost everything else. That there is a link between "getting it off your chest" and reduced cancer is fairly well established. [From the audiotape, "The Feeling Brain: Emotions and Health"]

Despite the subjectively evident (as well as clinically proven) fact that our emotions are integrally involved in governing our behavior and well-being, many people nevertheless ignore the importance of their emotions while striving for worldly success. There are "dress for success" and Image seminars, and video workshops that delineate proper personal presentation style. In every case the emphasis is on the exterior—the *outward manifestations* of success. These seminars and workshops will tell you what to say, how to stand, how to walk, how to dress, how to shake hands, and so on.

Engaging in these external "success" behaviors can work, but only if they generate the feelings of adequacy and competence that are needed to *congruently sustain* success in a given situation. The truth is that if your well-being does not emanate from *within* you, the result is an ongoing incongruity between what you are portraying on the outside and what you are experiencing on the inside. Rather than *being* confident, for instance, you may achieve a veneer of confidence, while unsettling and unpleasant emotions continue to churn and grate within. After taking their toll on your physical and mental well-being, sooner or later the effects of those unpleasant emotions work their way outside, affecting your behavior and revealing you as an imposter.

For many good reasons, you need to bring your life—including your emotions—under your control. We are not speaking here of the kind of control that people usually try to achieve, attempting to confine themselves to always responding in a certain positive way. That is not control; it is *being* controlled by your own rigidity. True control comes from having options about how to respond emotionally, and from having the ability to choose whichever of those options is most satisfying, given your current desires and circumstances. What is out of your control, what lies outside the arena of choice for you, can make your life miserable. Or even kill you.

## *Moving Toward Choice*

Looking back over the last week, month, or year you can probably find many examples of times when your feelings got in the way of being able to do what you wanted to do, being what you wanted to be, accomplishing what you wanted to accomplish. If you review your experiences of even the last few hours you will discover that your emotions make up much of your experience, and that your emotions, to a great extent, determine your responses. For instance, perhaps the anxiety or dread you felt about an upcoming meeting caused you to focus your planning on how to get out of the meeting or on how to handle the humiliation that it could lead to, rather than on planning the most effective presentation, as you would have done had you been feeling determined and anticipating success. Or maybe you felt shy and inadequate at a social gathering, and so you kept to yourself and interacted clumsily when others approached you, as contrasted with how you would have responded in that same situation if you had felt curious, capable, and attractive. Perhaps there have been times when you wanted to feel romantic, tender, and affectionate, but were actually feeling lethargic, and your relationship suffered as a result. Everyone can recall examples like these—times when what we felt was not useful.

Sometimes those nonuseful emotions are pleasant and sometimes not, but they are always with us: you angrily blow up at the kids when you would rather be understanding; you feel understanding and accepting of someone who has just taken advantage of you for the third time when you would rather be angry; you feel fearful of an impending interview when you would rather feel confident or hopeful; you feel discouraged about the prospects for a satisfying relationship when you would rather feel determined to make it happen.

After beating your head against your own emotional walls,

you may have come to believe that people have no choice about how they feel, and that much of life is simply coping with the fallout of emotions. It is our pleasure to tell you, however, that it definitely does not have to be that way. You *can* choose your emotions and, in so doing, have the kinds of experiences you want to have in your daily life.

How will you know when you are succeeding at developing emotional choice? To make the evidence of gaining and having choice more obvious to you, let us first contrast the manifestations of a *lack* of emotional choice.

There are three ways in which people demonstrate an inability to cope emotionally. The first is that they consistently and chronically respond to everyday or ongoing life situations with debilitating emotions, such as feeling inadequate, helpless, ashamed, despairing, angry, or frustrated. For some people the evening news, a teenager's punk haircut, a computer error on a bank statement, or being lied to are occasions for incapacitating emotions.

The second way people demonstrate a lack of emotional choice is by having no satisfying way to cope with emotions that they feel are intolerable, such as shyness, loneliness, inadequacy, fear, or guilt. Often they try to get away from those emotions by extreme withdrawal, by violence, or by using or abusing various substances.

Third, many people believe that it is *wrong* to feel certain emotions, such as desire, envy, anger, or irritation. Because of this belief, when they do experience one of these emotions they are plunged into feelings of shame or guilt.

But the same life situations that evoke debilitating emotions in some people evoke enviable responses in others. We all know people who not only cope well, but who thrive in situations in which we habitually find ourselves feeling and acting inappropriately. Those people are manifesting emotional choice, and they share two attributes.

The first attribute of emotional choice these people exhibit is responding with a wider range of emotions. Either they do not experience debilitating emotions in the first place; or if they do experience negative emotions, they don't dwell in them. The difference here is in terms of the *quantity* of and *ease of movement* among the emotions available to be experienced. It's like the difference between Foster's Freeze, where your choice is either chocolate or vanilla, and the thirty-one flavors of Baskin-Robbins. With a wide range of emotions on tap, such individuals do not dwell in a negative emotion any longer than they would keep eating a dish of seafood that tasted bad at first bite.

The second attribute of these individuals is that they respond to their emotions (both pleasant and unpleasant) as real and meaningful communications about how to make their lives better, rather than as random blows delivered by a hostile environment. Using their emotions as a means of taking the pulse of their well-being, they guide their attention and behaviors so as to provide themselves with desirable emotional experiences.

*You will be on your way to emotional choice when*

*You begin to appreciate that there is a wider range of emotions for you to experience*

*and*

*You begin to understand what each of your emotions is communicating to you*

This book is the culmination of our years of studying emotions and the means to access and sustain them. Through our studies we have learned how to choose, change, and use emotions to enrich our lives and the lives of those around us. What we learned we have turned into tools that anyone can use. You can create for yourself the emotional experiences that you want to have, when you want to have them. You are about to learn both how to choose the emotions you will experience, and how to express your emotions in a wide range of situations, in ways that are considerate of your own well-being and the well-being of others. With these tools comes freedom from debilitating emotions. With these tools comes the power to be your best.

3

# *Emotions Are the Source*

TO BUILD A WORLD IN WHICH HUMAN BEINGS ENJOY EMOtional choice, we must have a way of recognizing the basic material from which that world will be constructed—namely emotions. But recognizing emotions is not as automatic and obvious as many of us think.

As we have already hinted, emotions are not limited to a handful of common feelings, but include hundreds of distinctions. Though we may classify our emotions into broad categories, such as "positive," "negative," "pleasant," and "unpleasant," those classifications are not themselves emotions.

In one of our training seminars, Lisa, a high school principal, asked for help because she felt "bad." When we pressed her for more detail by asking, "What kind of 'bad'?", she could only respond, "You know, just bad." The fact was, however, that we *didn't* know, for "bad" is simply a name for a class of generally unpleasant emotions. After some examples of the differences between feeling bad and feeling worried or scared or inadequate, Lisa realized that the bad feeling she was experiencing was anxiety.

As Lisa discovered, emotions are distinct from the global classifications they may fall into, such as "good" or "bad." Knowing that you feel bad gives you almost no useful information about what is going on to make you feel that way, or what to do to change your situation. On the other hand, knowing precisely which emotion you are feeling provides you immediately with useful feedback. For instance, once we knew that Lisa was feeling anxiety, we knew that either her attention was focused on a future filled with unknowns, or that she felt ill-prepared to face some task or situation that held the possibility of unpleasant consequences, such as an upcoming confrontation with the school board. She needed to fill in the missing pieces and, if still necessary, she needed to take charge of that future situation by preparing to make it acceptable, desirable, or at least tolerable. Helping her simply amounted to assisting her in becoming adequately prepared to face that future. Once she realized that she was prepared to respond resourcefully in the future situation she was anticipating, her anxiety was replaced with feelings of self-assurance and confidence.

Emotions are not the same as the judgments we make about them, and neither are they the same as the behaviors they help generate. We have found that many people have only a few experiences coded as emotions, often limited to little more than fear, love, hate, joy, happiness, and sadness. The rest are merely descriptive words. But such things as responsibility, purposefulness, ambition, capability, confusion, frustration, pride, security, and affection are not only behaviors, but emotions as well. At times you *feel* responsible, *feel* purposeful, *feel* ambitious, and so on. The difference between running your experience through the sieve of a few all-purpose emotions and running it through the open floodgates of human experience is like the difference between black-and-white and color television, or between using only eight keys on a piano and using all eighty-eight.

There is often a difference between how a person is behaving and what he or she is feeling at the same time. For example, Leslie was often heard to say such things as, "Oh God, I have so much to do it's a wonder that I can manage to get it all done. But I have to be responsible!" This often-repeated declaration of hers, and the humorless way in which she said it, was a source of curiosity, so Michael asked her if she was *feeling* responsible. The question stopped Leslie cold. She blinked a few times, then answered wonderingly, "You know what? I don't. I just feel hassled!"

Leslie's realization may sound strange, but it is actually quite common. Sometimes we judge our experience by what we are doing—that is, by our behavior—forgetting that what we are doing and how we are feeling may be quite different. For instance, you might consider yourself a good socializer because you do fine at greeting people and making conversation, but meanwhile, inside you are feeling intimidated, or bored, or superior. You might see yourself as inadequate as you try to fathom the concepts presented in the physics course you are taking, overlooking the fact that you feel interested and determined. To notice and respond only to your behavior is to ignore a significant portion of your experience—your emotions.

The same is true when it comes to noticing and responding to others. There is often a difference between what you observe another person's behavior to be and what that person is feeling. This was demonstrated by a friend of ours whose teenage son had been acting sullen all afternoon. When our friend asked what was going on, he found out that the boy was feeling hurt because his friends had been teasing him. It would have been a mistake to assume from the boy's behavior that he was *feeling* sullen. He was not. The emotion he was feeling was "hurt," which for him manifested itself in what his father considered sullen *behavior.* Another common example of this point is the frenetic and boisterous behavior that children sometimes seem to get lost in, often incurring the wrath of their parents. Rather than *feeling* frenetic or boisterous, however, most often these kids are feeling lonely or left out. And they are responding to the need for connection that those feelings are signaling. Their feelings prompt them to seek whatever attention and contact they can get, even if it is abusive.

Of course, how a person feels will affect his behavior, and how a person behaves can affect how he feels, but nonetheless the two are distinct and may be quite different at any given moment.

This point is worth remembering because it is easy to assume that we know what is going on inside other people simply by watching their behavior. Our judgments in these cases may reveal something about how we behaviorally express our *own* emotions, but not be at all accurate when applied to the other person.

An emotion is an overall *feeling response* at a moment in time, and is different from the rational terms used to describe it. In *The Language of the Heart* (Basic Books, 1985), Dr. James J. Lynch documents the link between emotions and such physiological responses as blood pressure and heart rate. In a chapter titled "The Hidden Dialogue," he talks about how researchers at Massachusetts General Hospital discovered that many patients are either totally unaware of their feelings or can only describe them in rational, dissociated, nonfeeling terms. One of the doctors on the research team coined the term "alexithymic" to describe these individuals.

Typical of the problems alexithymic patients have when they are asked to articulate their feelings is the following case published by Dr. Nemiah and his colleagues:

> Related to the difficulties in describing feelings or localizing emotions is the fact that many patients *cannot distinguish among the different kinds of common affects.* [One patient], for example, when asked what it felt like to be frightened, replied: "What does it feel like to be frightened? (Pause.) I can't think of the term."

**Doctor:** "Do you feel it in your body?"
**Patient:** "I think it's mostly in your mind."
**Doctor:** "Your mind?"
**Patient:** "It's mostly in your head. Things go through your head."
**Doctor:** "It doesn't affect your body?"
**Patient:** "I don't . . . I can't say for sure. It might. It might. In the stomach maybe."
**Doctor:** "The stomach? And what would you feel there?"
**Patient:** "Knotted up in the stomach."
**Doctor:** "How does that differ from being mad?"
**Patient:** "How does it differ from being mad? Again, I . . . to me, to me all these things are in the same pot. You know, all in one pot."
**Doctor:** "They feel alike?"

**Patient:** "Yeah. The being scared, the being aggravated. To me it's from the head to the stomach . . . (long pause) I can't really . . . I'd like to say what you want to hear."

**Doctor:** "I want to hear what you feel, that's all."

**Patient:** "Yeah, well . . . I can't really say." [pp. 233–234]

Because people who are "blind" to their emotions have no way of understanding their blindness, their misleading use of language often prevents others from detecting the problem. Communication problems and misunderstandings are rampant.

> Those individuals who have normal color vision, for example, take their perception of colors for granted, while those who are color-blind have no idea what they have missed. Color blindness frequently goes undetected because one cannot miss a phenomenon one has never experienced. Confusion about the problem is compounded by the fact that the color-blind individual knows there are words such as *red*, *yellow*, and *green* and is perfectly capable of using these color words in sentences without ever having seen or experienced the colors. So, too, everyone knows such words as *love*, *hate*, *jealousy*, *ecstasy*, and *envy*, and everyone can use these words when talking to others. There is, however, a marked difference between *rationally using feeling terms* that one has never experienced, and using these same terms when one has experienced—that is, felt—the emotions these terms designate. Psychosomatic patients can wax eloquent with operational fact-filled descriptions of various human emotions even though they have no idea of how these emotions feel.
>
> The problem becomes increasingly exacerbated the more intense one's feeling become. Strong emotional arousal creates especially serious problems for alexithymic individuals. Unable to describe their own feelings, they also lose the capacity to discriminate between and among the bodily correlates of various feelings. An intense surge of blood pressure could just as easily be a storm of hatred or a tidal wave of love. Alexithymic patients have no real way of telling the difference. [pp. 234–235]

Dr. Lynch usually asks, "How are you feeling?" at the beginning of every session as his patient is being attached to machines that monitor blood pressure, heart rate, and so on. The response of alexithymic patients is obviously frustrating and exasperating to him.

> The patient quickly shifts the topic, moving out of the feeling domain, back toward the security of the cognitive realm, the safe realm of thought and reason, by answering, "I think I'm okay." At the same moment, the patient's blood pressure or heart rate frequently increases 25 percent to 50 percent. Such patients answer questions about their feelings in a rational way that exacts a physical cost. When Patty once so blandly answered questions about her feelings, I exclaimed in some exasperation, "I know *how* you *think*, and *what* you *think*, and *why* you *think*, and *when* you *think*, and *where* you *think*, but I asked you *how do you feel?—not how you think.*"
>
> She smiled at the outburst and again replied, "What do you mean how do I feel today? I just told you that I'm okay."
>
> "I mean are you angry, or sad, or joyful, or enraged, or loving?"
>
> Again she smiled and sighed, "I think I am okay." [pp. 237–238]

Even though an emotion is an *overall feeling response* at a given moment, it should not be confused with the set of body sensations that you may also be feeling. The "knotted up in the stomach" reply in the first doctor/patient interview above is an example of a body sensation. It's not an emotion. We recently worked with a client who responded to the question, "What are you feeling?" with "I feel like I'm moving slow, it's an effort to even lift my hand. My head feels heavy, and I feel a kind of emptiness in my stomach." She was describing the various *body* feelings that she was experiencing, rather than the emotion of which those body sensations were a part. We had intended to find out what emotion she was feeling, but instead of answering the question we intended, she had answered the one we asked: "What are you feeling?" Correcting ourselves, we then asked her, "What *emotion* are you feeling?" and after a moment's thought she answered, "Depressed. I feel depressed."

Thus there is a difference between the sensations that involve parts of your body and *your overall subjective experience of the moment*, or "emotion." It is important to be able to distinguish between your emotions and your "part-body" feelings so that you know better how to respond to what is going on with you. For instance, it turned out that our depressed client experienced those same part-body sensations when she was physically fatigued. (She would know that she was "depressed" if she was longing to go to sleep in order to escape, but that she was "fatigued" if she was happy to be going to sleep.) Obviously, if you are depressed you will need to respond differently to your situation than if you are fatigued.

*Emotions are our global subjective responses at a given moment.*

*Emotions are distinct from part-body feelings that may be going on at the same time.*

*Emotions are distinct from the behaviors they help generate.*

*Emotions are distinct from the value judgments we make about them.*

## Emotions Are Messages

To some people, emotional choice would mean being able to pick those emotions they enjoy or find enriching or enlivening, and to live their lives accompanied always by those chosen pleasant feelings. But if you succeeded at doing that, what would you really be letting yourself in for?

If you could choose right now, which six emotions would you like to experience for the rest of your life, and which six would you do away with? (It will be worth your while to stop and answer this question before reading on. When you have finished this book it will be instructive to return here and see how your answers have changed.)

| EXPERIENCE | DISCARD |
| --- | --- |
| __________ | __________ |
| __________ | __________ |
| __________ | __________ |
| __________ | __________ |
| __________ | __________ |
| __________ | __________ |

No matter what you put down on either of the above lists, you are probably cheating yourself. For instance, it's unlikely that you included "disappointment" or "frustration" on your list of desirable emotions. And yet disappointment lets you know that you did not get something that you wanted and expected that was important to you. Like disappointment, frustration involves not getting some outcome that you wanted and expected. The difference is that when you are frustrated *you are still holding the possibility of achieving your outcome and you are still pursuing it.* Disappointment signals that the possibility of getting "it" is over, and the response is to let go, to quit; the response to frustration is to *keep pursuing.*

For instance, think of something that you wanted during the last year, but did not get. Indulge for a few moments in being disappointed about not getting it. Now consider: Do you still want whatever it was that you didn't get? If you don't still want it, find something else to be disappointed about, something that you *do* still want. Once you have such an example, rather than continuing to feel disappointed, indulge for a few moments in the realization that you *can* get it; it is something you still want, and it is possible for you to get it, you are trying to get it, but the ways in which you are trying just aren't working. In other words, feel frustrated about not having it. How is feeling frustrated different from feeling disappointed? Again, the answer that we invariably get when we pose that question is that when people are frustrated they still feel engaged in striving toward getting whatever it is they want even though they may not know exactly what to do in order to succeed.

Disappointment is useful for getting yourself to let go of an outcome, accept it, and move on to other more productive endeavors. It may be very appropriate to be disappointed that an aquaintance still will not give up drugs after you have done everything you can and are willing to do no more. Or if your child hates taking ballet lessons despite your encouragement and support, it's appropriate to feel disappointment, then to accept the fact and move on to other more appropriate possibilities for both of you.

Frustration keeps you striving. Unless you think there is nothing more you can do, it is appropriate to feel frustrated with your child's behavior problems, or with communication problems between you and your mate, or with the fact that your health is not as good as you would like it to be. If it is worth feeling frustrated about, then it is worth accessing the emotions of patience and determination to see the task through to the end. The worth of an emotion, then, cannot be measured by how pleasant it is to experience, but only by the outcome it is intended to serve.

## *Functional Attributes*

Imagine that you are watching two close friends of yours, Jim and Linda. You love and respect them both, and you know that they care deeply about each other. As you watch, you overhear Jim pleading with Linda to heed his advice. Jim's pleas are delivered with such heartfelt urgency and intensity that they sound like demands. It is obvious to you that his "demands" are motivated by his real concern and caring for Linda. Linda, however, just stands there, ignoring Jim and everything that he is saying.

Now shift your perspective and imagine that you are in Jim's shoes. You know that your friend Linda is in need of help and guidance. She is about to make a terrible mistake by ignoring warning signs—in a relationship, or in an investment, or in her job perhaps—signs that are obvious to you but that she is oblivious to. You are the only one who can keep her from being hurt. You are more than concerned, you are desperate to help her. You implore, you reach out and take her hands in yours and plead, but your pleas fall on deaf ears. Linda just stands there, looking away, ignoring you.

Finally, shift your perspective again so that now you are in Linda's place. You are the person who is unaware that an important message is being ignored. A good friend, a wise friend, a friend who has your best interests at heart, is begging you to listen. Your friend is pleading and even demanding that you do what is necessary to protect your well-being. But this time there is one change in the scenario. The concerned, wise friend making those pleas and demands is *your emotions.*

Your emotions are like a caring friend who is letting you know about a situation that you really need to respond to. Also, like a caring friend, your emotions may be letting you know about something that is unpleasant; they may even be giving you information in a way that's painful to hear. Nevertheless, it would be foolish to ignore what your emotional friend is trying to tell you.

No matter how unpleasant an emotion seems to be, it is actually worth having as a *signal*. What that signal is about—what that emotion is trying to tell you—we call the "functional attribute" of the emotion. Even the most unpleasant emotions have functional attributes that can be useful if you respond to them as important messages about your needs. The first step in utilizing your emotions is to recognize what they are signaling you about. The second step is to respond properly to that message. Let's look at some examples.

The functional attribute of *regret* is that it points out *what you could have or should have done differently in some past situation.* You might regret not having studied for an exam that you flunked, or that you said unkind things to your mother when you were a teenager, or that you declined an invitation and later found out that you missed out on a fabulous time and certain romantic opportunities. Whatever your personal regrets, and however painful they may be, it is important to realize that that feeling is letting you know you made a mistake. Only through recognizing your mistakes can you avoid repeating them in the future.

The functional attribute of *guilt* is that it signals that *you have violated a personal standard and that you need to make sure not to do it again in the future.* For instance, you may feel guilty that you lied to a friend; or you forgot a promise you made to your child; or you didn't take a stand, but stood by while something you considered unjust took place. No one likes to feel guilty, but when you do, it is feedback to you that you have violated, or are thinking of violating, an important personal standard of yours. If you did not have that kind of feedback, there would be little to keep your behavior in line with your standards.

The functional attribute of *anxiety* is that it lets you know that *there is something in your future for which you need to prepare better.* You might feel anxious about making a large financial commitment at a time when your job security is uncertain; or about going to a party where you won't know anyone; or when you have to go in for an IRS audit. The feeling of anxiety makes you aware of the need to either prepare for these situations or to avoid them altogether. Occasional feelings of anxiety keep you from recreating on a daily basis your own personal version of the Battle of the Little Big Horn.

Feeling *overwhelmed* is usually the result of attempting to achieve outcomes that are too imposing or too numerous to be accomplished in the time you have available. The functional attribute of feeling overwhelmed is that it is a signal to you that *you need to reevaluate and set priorities on the tasks you have set for yourself.* So, you have to plan and shop for a party, pick the children up at school and take them to the doctor, clean the house, get the tires balanced, and cook dinner—all before the PTA meeting at 7 o'clock this evening. That feeling of being overwhelmed is a notice to step back from your tower of tasks and make some decisions about which tasks are necessary and which are not, and the order in which they should be tackled.

When your well-being is endangered by the appearance of a rival for the attentions and affections of someone close to you, the most usual response is to feel jealous. The functional attribute of *jealousy* is that it points out to you that *you believe that your emotional well-being is in jeopardy and you need to do something.* You may feel jealous when you notice your mate tucked into a corner of the room at a party with an attractive member of the opposite sex, engrossed in conversation and seemingly oblivious to your presence. Or perhaps your mate has been working late, night after night, with an attractive colleague. Such situations could threaten the well-being of your relationship and therefore your personal well-being. The feeling of jealousy alerts you to the possibility of these threats. If you did not feel jealous, then you might allow a threatening situation to evolve to a point where your relationship was irreparably damaged.

When someone threatens your well-being, either intentionally or unintentionally, you probably respond by feeling angry. The functional attribute of *anger* is that it lets you know that *you need to do something to stop the abuse of your well-being, or to prevent it in the future.* Perhaps you discovered that you were cheated in the financing of your car; or that your supervisor misrepresented you to another supervisor; or that a friend has lied to you. The anger that you may feel at such times is a notice to you that someone has done something that has harmed you. If that notice were not posted, you would not do anything to ensure that similar harm did not come to you in the future. Nor would those who have harmed you be likely to become aware of the pain they have inflicted and so have an opportunity to make amends—both to you and to themselves.

The functional attribute is the very heart of emotion utilization because, once it is specified for a particular emotion, it immediately transforms that emotion into a feeling worth having and using. It is worthwhile to know when you have made a mistake, violated your own standards, or are still striving toward an outcome, *provided* becoming aware of those things becomes the impetus for responding to them appropriately.

Too often, however, emotions are *felt and expressed but not responded to.* There is little point in regretting something you have done unless that feeling of regret helps you change your future behavior. There is little point in feeling guilty unless your feeling of guilt leads to a renewal of will and intention to fulfill your standards in the future. There is little point in feeling frustrated unless that feeling of frustration propels you toward creative efforts to attain your desired outcome. The functional attribute of an unpleasant emotion *specifies what you need to do to respond appropriately to that emotion.*

Unpleasant emotions are worth having if they are used well. For instance, if you believe in everyone being personally responsible for keeping the environment clean, it is appropriate to feel guilty when you realize that you have left some trash behind at your campsite. Similarly, it is understandable if you feel angry when you discover that someone else has left trash blowing about the campsite. In fact, if you could not have these emotions you would be at a great disadvantage. If you never felt overwhelmed you might easily squander your time working on outcomes that are actually of a low priority. The inability to feel jealous could turn you into someone for whom relationships are interchangeable and easily replaceable. And if you never felt angry you could easily be mistaken for a doormat. When seen in the light of their signal value, even terribly unpleasant emotions gain a quality that makes them worth having—especially when they propel you toward useful outcomes and behaviors.

## *Gaining Emotional Choice*

Now that you have some idea of what we mean by "emotions" and their functional attributes, we can take a few steps back and better describe what we mean when we talk about "emotional choice." True emotional choice means possessing and using the four abilities discussed in the following sections:

*Placement*
*Expression*
*Employment*
*Prevention*

## *Placement*

The first key to emotional choice is the ability to consistently respond to life's situations with those emotions that are most appropriate and useful. You have appropriate "placement" of your emotions when you are using the most appropriate emotion for each context in your life.

An example of appropriate placement is feeling disappointment instead of frustration when you have done everything you can to help a recalcitrant friend on drugs. In this situation it may be most appropriate first to feel disappointment, then to let go of the intense personal involvement and to move instead to acceptance or possibly to a passive *hope* that the person may change in the future without your help. Or if it is not appropriate to withdraw your personal involvement, you could extend further into the future the time at which you expect your friend to be off drugs, thus allowing you to move to patience. Any of these options would be better for both of you than hanging in there feeling frustrated. Other examples of contexts in which disappointment is an appropriate emotional response include recognizing that a relationship has gone irretrievably bad, or letting another person live her life the way she chooses, even if you can see it leading nowhere good. Other types of appropriate placement include feeling determined instead of discouraged in order to maintain a commitment to accomplishing a long-term goal, or feeling capable instead of inadequate as you undertake a new endeavor.

All of us occasionally respond to a certain situation with an emotion other than what we need or would like in that situation. Having recognized that his emotional response is inappropriate or debilitating, the person with emotional choice can identify what emotion(s) would serve better, then move into having that emotion when needed. For instance, such a person would recognize the need to step out of his frustration and into disappointment and then on to acceptance of his child's adamant disinterest in football, in dance lessons, or in eventually attending his alma mater.

After being stung a few times, Leslie appropriately contextualized some of her emotions by changing how she feels during negotiations from generous and helpful, to feeling cautious and careful about what she is committing to. Whenever Michael begins to feel skeptical about our son's sincerity, he moves to feeling trusting and supportive instead, both to give Mark the experience of being trusted and trustworthy, and for Michael to be able to feel at ease and loving.

In order to be able to select the appropriate emotions in relation to your needs in a particular situation, you must have some knowledge of the properties of various emotions and the behaviors they lead to, as well as an idea of what you would like to get out of that particular situation.

## *Expression*

The second key to emotional choice is the ability to choose how to *express* a given emotion. It is most desirable to express a given emotion in a way that is congruent with your concept of self and with the outcome you desire. Expressing emotions in ways that are incompatible with who you are can only lead to an uncomfortable and possibly detrimental incongruity that will be detected not only by you, but by those around you as well.

While quality of emotional expression is relevant to all emotions, it is especially important when you are expressing an emotion toward another person, such as anger, affection, appreciation, disappointment, annoyance, sympathy, frustration, or admiration. There is little point in expressing emotion toward another person unless your expression of that emotion conveys the meaning and impact that you want it to. For instance, expressing appreciation to someone by being overly gushy may lead the recipient of your appreciation to perceive you as insincere. Expressing anger through destructive behavior could destroy the very relationship you find important enough to get angry about—or even land you in jail. Expressing affection with sexual behavior could, in certain situations, lead to grave misunderstanding, and anything but affection.

Of course, there are times when it is most suitable to be *in*congruent and to have a range of choices about how to express yourself. For instance, lawyers and businesspeople involved in negotiations may want at times to portray cool confidence, even though their insides are churning with doubt or anxiety. In any case, the goal is to have a means of detecting what emotion you are experiencing and then (unless you choose to move to another emotion entirely) choosing how you would prefer to express that emotion in the future.

Suppose for example, that your teenage son carries on interminable telephone conversations in the kitchen, and that these marathons disrupt your peace of mind and your thought processes, intrude on your experience with chaotic sensations and tempos, and leave you feeling annoyed. Regardless of what else you might attempt to concentrate on, your annoyance persists. Rather than move to a different emotional response (such as tolerance or acceptance), you could turn to a useful and appropriate means of expressing that annoyance.

A woman we know who found herself in this very situation used to let her annoyance build up inside of her until she lashed out at her son, screaming things at him that later made her feel ashamed. Her family saw her as harsh and irrational, while her son got to act martyred and reasonable. When she discovered that she could choose how to express her annoyance creatively, she took to growling like a puma or a wild dog, giving a warning to her son when she felt that his telephone time had become excessive. This proved far more effective (if a bit eccentric) than screaming, banging down the telephone receiver, whining to her husband, or nagging her son. When she growled, the rest of the family—including her son—became immediately alert and attentive to what they might be doing to cause such a response. (It should be noted that the family members also desired to be spared the experience of screaming, nagging, and whining.)

In the first chapter we described how Michael, to his detriment and to the dismay of those around him, would express feelings of hurt or anger by withdrawing. Now he is quick to speak his concerns adamantly, and even to yell now and then. This expression is much more effective for him, and is not only preferred by his family and friends, but is appreciated as well. Now that they have the opportunity as soon as he becomes upset to know why he is upset, they can immediately offer reassurances, give explanations, make amends, or engage in a healthy argument. Through a change in expression, long painful ordeals have given way to brief storms.

Expression can also be used as a tool to enhance enjoyable emotions. Using Michael again as an example, his business partners were often confounded by his response to his financial successes. They would be close to jumping up and down with excitement when a piece of property was sold and they had made a substantial amount of money. Michael wanted to join his partners in feeling joyous, but usually he would feel only a mild and quickly fading satisfaction. To Michael, *buying* property in a way that ensured money would be made was a challenge and an art. To others, the sale of the property months or years later was the *realization* of profits and cause for celebration. For Michael the sale was anticlimactic, simply a confirmation of his initial judgment; in his mind the profits had been realized through the selection and structure of the purchase. His thrill came when he bought property. Yet he deserved to be able to feel more than fleeting satisfaction when a sale was consummated. His new understanding of the effect on emotions of different expressions enabled him to come up with a more enjoyable response. Now he expresses his feelings of satisfaction at financial successes by purchasing gifts for friends—computers, books, trips—that he knows will help his friends attain successes of their own. Their surprise adds fuel to his satisfaction, and the spark of their delight ignites his feelings into a blaze of joy that warms and brightens; and that joy is reignited and enjoyed anew each time that gift helps them in some way to make progress toward the achievement of their dreams.

## *Employment*

The third key to emotional choice is the ability to utilize unpleasant emotional states to generate useful behaviors, and to lead to more pleasurable emotions as well. The first step toward fully employing your emotions is being able to identify the functional attribute of an emotion—that is, to identify what a particular emotion is good for or what it signals. As we discussed earlier, no matter how unpleasant an emotion may be to experience, it always serves some function. Choice comes from the ability to recognize that function and then to respond to it by addressing whatever need is inherent in its signal. Part of addressing the need is selecting, accessing, and sustaining a different emotion—one that facilitates the fulfillment of that particular need.

Once identified, the functional attribute can be used to change your feelings and behaviors in desired ways. Rather than *needing* to get rid of unpleasant feelings, you have the choice of respecting them as important expressions of, and feedback about, your experience, and then using those emotions to take you to useful next steps.

For example, most people are familiar with the unpleasant spin of anxiety. Feeling anxious can seem like an inescapable trap, tightening its grip with each effort on your part to struggle free. It is an emotion so dreaded, in fact, that many people spend a great deal of time feeling anxious about the next time they are going to feel anxious, which they know could be any time soon. But the unknown or expected unpleasant future that can result in anxiety is the very thing that points the way out of anxiety and toward reassurance and confidence. Anxiety is a signal that there is something waiting in your future for which you need to better prepare. That preparation may consist of simply gathering more information in order to fill in an incomplete picture of the "who, what, where, when, and why" of some future event. Leslie uses anxiety in two ways to better prepare for the future.

She has learned that anxiety can be a signal that when she is thinking about an upcoming event, she is imagining only one possibility: it will be unpleasant. For instance, if she is scheduled to give a presentation to the training staff of a corporation, she might only make mental pictures in which she is awkward, forgets what she planned to say, elicits negative responses in her audience, and so on. If that kind of nightmare is the only possibility you consider, you are writing your own ticket for a trip to anxiety prison—do not pass Go. Realizing this, when Leslie begins to feel anxious about a presentation (or any other type of situation) these days, she recognizes that feeling as a signal that she needs to create pictures of future possibilities that are positive and reassuring. She does this by asking and answering the questions, "What do I *want* to have happen?" and "What can I do to ensure, as nearly as possible, that what I want to have happen will happen?" Once she identifies what she needs to do, and how it will work to bring about the future she wants, she uses her past to confirm that she is capable of doing each step. After that, she rehearses putting her plan into effect, all the while picturing the desired future unfolding. In this way she uses the first twinges of anxiety as a springboard to curiosity about positive possibilities, reassurance based on past experience, and confidence about her future.

However, she is not always successful in finding ways to eliminate the likelihood of an unpleasant future experience. When feelings of anxiety persist despite her best efforts at changing her pictures of the future into positive ones, she understands those feelings as a signal that she needs to assess the actual risk involved. She asks and answers questions such as, "What's really at stake here? My life? My health? An important relationship? Money? My credibility? Rejection? A few hours of unpleasantness? Anything of real importance?" Usually she discovers that she is risking, at most, possible rejection by people who are not in a position to diminish her life and whose rejection would not be significant a few years from now. And often she discovers that she is risking only a few hours of discomfort. Once identified, the anxiety disappears and instead she feels informed, resigned, and accepting of the nominal risks.

### *Prevention*

The fourth key to emotional choice is the ability to influence your personal behavior and life situations in order to prevent certain immobilizing and dreadful emotions—or even milder unpleasant emotions if you so choose. Overwhelmingly harsh emotions such as rage, shame, humiliation, terror, and utter helplessness, although possessing functional attributes, are generally so debilitating that they are worth preventing whenever possible.

Prevention of such an overpowering emotion involves first identifying the circumstances that trigger it and then either changing your behavior with respect to that emotion or reorganizing your life situations to prevent the triggering of that emotion. Take as an example someone who always feels humiliated on the dance floor. This person can either remove himself from the triggering situation by avoiding dances and parties, or he can engage in behavior that prevents it from happening by learning to dance well enough to avoid feeling humiliated. The person who feels helpless when confronted by her overbearing boss at work can identify what she needs in order to feel powerful around the boss and adopt those perceptions and acquire those behaviors; or she can remove herself from the situation by finding another job with a more congenial superior. There are many ways to foster your well-being, including changing the way you think, your behavior, or your life situation.

These four abilities—placement, expression, employment, and prevention—are explored more fully in the following chapters. And those chapters also contain a bonus. As you gain emotional choice by learning the specific techniques that lead to the mastery of these abilities, you will become more adept at recognizing the emotions other people are experiencing, and how to use that information in deciding how to respond to them. How you choose to respond will include considerations about whether you want to enhance or change the emotion that another person is feeling. If you want to help change his or her emotion, then you will be better prepared than before to do just that. Your responses to others will be a matter of choice, rather than a reaction.

For instance, if you realize that your daughter is feeling insecure, you could respond by worrying, too, and perhaps end up increasing the child's insecurity. Or you can recognize that when people are feeling insecure they are asking for reassurance. Your task, then, is to find out what kind of reassurance you can give your child so that she can move from feeling insecure to feeling secure. (You will not always be right in your assessment of what is needed, of course, but since you now know where you are going in terms of an emotion, you will be able to get there eventually.)

Take as another example the discovery that your wife is enjoying feeling satisfied. Satisfaction contains no inherent request and there is probably no need to change it to some other emotion. So what does it have to do with you? Well, how about *enhancing* her satisfaction, perhaps by enjoying it with her?

THE FOUR KEY ABILITIES OF EMOTIONAL CHOICE

| | |
|---|---|
| *Placement* | The ability to respond to life's situations with emotions that are appropriate and useful |
| *Expression* | The ability to choose how to express emotions |
| *Employment* | The ability to utilize unpleasant emotions to generate useful behaviors and pleasant emotions |
| *Prevention* | The ability to prevent yourself from experiencing certain overwhelming and immobilizing emotions |

## *What This Book Delivers*

This book will not do away with your emotions. Instead, it will enrich your experience of them, giving you the ability to recognize and use your emotions for your own well-being and the well-being of others, as well as the ability to move to useful and desirable behaviors in order to accomplish your personal outcomes. This journey of discovery and acquisition begins in earnest in the next chapter, which introduces the *structure of emotions*.

We are confident that the information and illustrative examples that you need to fufill the promise of this book are contained in these pages. But there is something that you will need in addition to that information and those examples: your participation. The following chapters contain thought and feeling experiments for you to engage in. These are more than mere illustrations of the point being made—they are intended to be *learning experiences*. We want this book to benefit you not only intellectually, but experientially as well. In order for that to happen, it is necessary for you to immerse yourself in the explorations we have provided for you.

You may not wish to interrupt your reading in order to carry out an exercise. We strongly encourage that, if you do choose to read on past an exercise without doing it, at the conclusion of that section or chapter you return and take yourself through the exercises before moving on.

You have already embarked on a journey that we expect you will find fascinating, useful, and worthwhile. In these first three chapters you have already taken more steps than you may have been aware of, and perhaps the most difficult ones of the journey as well.

# 4

# *The Structure of Emotions*

EMOTIONS ARE REAL. WE ALL EXPERIENCE THEM, AND THEY regularly effect impressive changes in our behaviors and our physiologies. But where do emotions come from? Thin air? Do we just suddenly feel apprehensive or joyous, or do we feel these things in certain circumstances? Often we attribute our emotional states to external circumstances. For instance, you are turned down for a date and feel humiliated, or you get a job and feel joyous, or you are assigned to do a presentation for the boss and feel apprehensive. It often seems that the situation dictates our emotions. But if we look around we discover that there are some people who feel disdainful or accepting rather than humiliated when turned down for a date; who feel apprehensive rather than joyous when offered a job; and who feel challenged rather than apprehensive when facing a presentation for the boss. *Your emotions, then, are not determined by the circumstances, but by what is going on inside you in relation to those circumstances.*

What is going on inside you are certain perceptions and thought processes, which at a given moment determine what you are feeling. Let's say that your emotions are analogous to the atmosphere at a party. Depending upon the particular mix of people who are there, the party will take on certain characteristics—quiet, relaxing, raucous, intimate, cold, and so on. When someone leaves or arrives the mix changes, and the entire tenor of the party may change dramatically. Whether it is Mr. Gregarious showing up at a party of wallflowers, Ms. Bore leaving, or the Loud Family descending, the atmosphere of the party will change in some way. Your perceptions and thought processes are like the people attending the party. As they take on various characteristics (like guests coming and going) so do your emotions change (as does the atmosphere of the party).

Similarly, the particular characteristics of a molecule will change as its arrangement of atoms is changed or as various atoms are stripped from or bonded to it. For example, if you rearrange the molecules that give caraway seeds their flavor so that they have the same atoms but arranged in a mirror image of the caraway molecule, the result is a molecule that tastes like spearmint. Chloroform is highly flammable, but an added atom of chlorine creates carbon tetrachloride, which will extinguish flames. And adding oxygen molecules to the alcohol in wine produces vinegar. Just as the properties of a molecule are determined by the arrangement and kinds of atoms that go into it, our emotions are determined by the particular mix of perceptions and thought processes we are engaging in at a particular moment.

Emotions have components, just like a party (its guests) or a molecule (its atoms). For each of us any given emotion will certainly carry our own individual stamp; but it is also true that some components of the emotion are the same for any person experiencing that emotion. Those components of an emotion that are the same for all of us are the ones that are most responsible for imbuing that emotion with its particular characteristics and impact (like the atmosphere of a party, or the properties of a molecule). This cultural uniformity of the components of emotions makes it possible to understand and pattern the things we feel in a way that leads to having choices about our emotions.

Here is an experiential example of what we are talking about.

Think of some very unpleasant emotion that you have experienced within the last year. Just think of it, don't reexperience it.

Now *hope* that you will never feel that emotion again. Feel that hope completely, then pay attention to how you know you are "hoping." In other words, how do you know it is hope that you are experiencing?

Now step away from that experience and begin to *anticipate* that you will never feel that emotion again. Feel this anticipation completely. Then attend to what "anticipating" is like, and how you know that you are anticipating.

Here are some examples of things you might anticipate and hope: *anticipate* that your child or spouse will be coming home, or that you will have social security to rely on when you retire, or that you will make love tonight. Then, *hope* that your child or spouse will come home, that social security will still be around when you retire, or that you will get to make love tonight. Notice in what ways your experience changes when you go from anticipation to hope. Now try *hoping* that there will be no nuclear war, or that your marriage will last; then *anticipate* that there will be no nuclear war, or that your marriage will last. How does going from hope to anticipation affect your experience?

What is the difference between hoping and anticipating for you? People invariably do find significant differences. The typical response is, "When I anticipate it's for sure, but when I hope it's not for sure. Also, I feel more engaged or involved when I'm anticipating something."

How is it possible that anticipating seems certain and involving, while hoping seems uncertain and passive? What makes one qualitatively different from the other? While there are many possible differences between these two emotions, the most significant of the subjective components for hope and anticipation are as follows. (You will learn more about these and other components soon.)

| ***Anticipation*** | ***Hope*** |
|---|---|
| *Sense of actively moving toward the imagined outcome or object of anticipation* | *Sense of passively waiting for the imagined outcome* |
| *Imagine only one possibility/ outcome* | *Imagine both what is being hoped for and what is hoped will not happen* |

In creating the emotions of anticipation and of hope, the items in these two lists are just like the particular mix of guests at a party or the particular arrangement of atoms in a molecule. That unique set of guests makes up the structure of the party, and that specific arrangement of atoms makes up the structure of the molecule. In precisely the same way, the components listed above (and others we will mention in the next chapter) make up the *structure* of the emotions of anticipation and hope.

The items listed above are the most significant ones differentiating anticipation from hope. When we hope for something we maintain a dual image of what might happen, an image in which we hold before us simultaneously both the possibility of things turning out the way we want them to *and* the possibility of things not turning out the way we want them to. When we anticipate, however, we hold before us the image of only one possible outcome—whether it's an outcome that we want, or an outcome that we don't want.

If these differences were not evident to you from the exercise you just did, here is another way to experience them. Begin by thinking of something that you are currently anticipating, such as getting a raise at work. Once you have that image in mind, at the same time imagine whatever you are anticipating *not* happening—for example, both getting the raise and not getting the raise. What happens to your anticipation? Next, consider something that you are currently hoping for, then eliminate all but one of the possibilities that you have been considering. What happens to your hope?

Hope and anticipation are subjectively and structurally different from one another. And as you have just demonstrated for yourself, adopting into your own experience those characteristic structures *creates* in you the feeling of either hope or anticipation. The behaviors that result from these emotions are different as well. The subjective response to anticipation is that something in the future is "for sure." This emotion therefore orients you toward preparing for that future. The uncertain nature of hope, however, often leaves you unsure about what to do in relation to the future. For instance, many people who hope for peace actually do little about attaining it. In hoping for peace they are imagining both the possibility of peace and the possibility of war. When both futures seem equally possible, the person may be left unsure about whether to work for peace or to prepare for war.

Similarly, perhaps you know someone who is always hoping for a raise while at the same time doing nothing to persuade her boss to agree to it. On the other hand, people who anticipate getting a raise are confident of the outcome and actively pursue it or prepare to spend it. Because only the one possibility is being imagined—whether it is getting the raise, raking in big profits from an investment, or winning a prize—some people even spend their imagined windfall in advance, often with tragic consequences. Hope and anticipation are different structurally, and that difference usually results in very different behaviors. How many people do you think would clear a room in their house, repaint or wallpaper it, buy a bed they could never sleep in, and stock up on diapers and baby powder if, instead of anticipating the birth of a child, they only hoped for it?

Another example of the underlying structure of emotions can be found in the differences between frustration and disappointment. To experience this difference in structure for yourself, think of some recent disappointment (you didn't get a raise, you saw no improvement in your child's behavior, you had a terrible time on a date), and *feel* that disappointment now. As you feel that disappointment, again want what you originally wanted, pretending that you can still have it. How does doing that change your emotion?

Now think of something you feel frustrated about (perhaps not getting a raise, not seeing an improvement in your child's behavior, or not having a good time on a date), and *feel* that frustration. As you feel that frustration, pretend that it is now not possible to get what you wanted. How does doing that change your emotion?

Frustration and disappointment are both emotions you might feel when you are not getting something you want. Whether you feel one emotion or the other depends largely on whether or not you continue to hold an image of the future in which the possibility of getting what you want still exists. If you continue to want "it" and continue to believe that it is somehow possible to get "it," then you will feel frustrated and probably do something about getting what you want. If instead you let go of the possibility of getting what you want, then you will feel disappointed—the opportunity to get what you wanted no longer exists in your future. With disappointment something is "over" and you tend to disengage yourself from whatever it was that you wanted, while frustration is based on the belief that you can still get what you want, and so keeps you striving toward your goal.

## *Understanding Structure*

In this chapter we have introduced the observation that the characteristics of each emotion are the result of particular sets of perceptual components, which make up the individual structures of those emotions.

What makes emotional choice possible is knowing and being able to respond usefully to the structure of emotions. We are confident that once you give it a try, you will find it to be a fascinating, sensible, and even familiar experience. Nevertheless, we do want to be sure that you appreciate the significant role that understanding structure plays in your being able to respond out of choice rather than routine. The following three points are important to that understanding.

### 1. *Knowing the structure of emotions leads to appropriateness.*

It is not enough to simply have access to even a wide range of emotions. As we have illustrated, an emotion may be either appropriate or not, depending upon the situation in which you are feeling it. In addition, inappropriate emotions can lead to immobilization, unwanted behaviors, and unnecessarily unfortunate outcomes. By knowing the structure of emotions, however, you can determine when—that is, in what situations—a particular emotion is "better" than another.

For example, knowing what you now know about the structural differences between hope and anticipation, you can be more conscious about when to step into those feelings. You can anticipate summer while shivering through the winter, anticipate your retirement while shuffling through the papers on your overloaded desk, anticipate the need to be rested for the long day you will have to put in tomorrow, or anticipate the birth of your child. However, you will want to hope for those things that are out of your control and that you are unwilling to be involved in making happen. You can hope that the three-toed salamanders will be saved, hope that the tribal dances of an obscure New Guinea tribe will be preserved, and hope that your child will be accepted by the school of her dreams.

All of us can identify many situations in which, despite our best intentions to the contrary, we consistently respond with emotions that lead us into reacting and behaving in ways that are not at all what we want. Understanding how the stucture of emotions compels your experiences and behaviors allows you to become purposeful about fulfilling your wants and needs.

### 2. *Knowing structure makes it possible to change your emotions.*

Being "trapped in an emotion" is a common experience. You start feeling a certain way and, even though you want to change how you feel—and even though you know what you *do* want to feel—you simply can't seem to break free of the emotion that has engulfed you. A common example of this is the emotion of jealousy. You know intellectually that you have nothing to feel jealous about, and you can tell that your jealous behavior is jeopardizing your relationship, but you still can't manage to not feel jealous.

You need not be trapped by your emotions, however. By knowing the structure of the emotions you are in and, more important, the structure of the emotions you would like to move into, *you can choose to create for yourself the perceptions that will lead to the emotions you prefer.* In fact, if you have engaged in the exercises in this chapter, you have already done this at least a couple of times.

By learning about the structure of emotions, you will be able to change your emotions from one to another, and in this way affect both the quality of your experience and the character of your behavior.

### 3. *Knowing structure makes all emotional states available to you.*

Using the example of disappointment and frustration, we illustrated that unpleasant and unwanted emotions may nevertheless be important and useful. The person who has access to disappointment but not to frustration may find himself chronically giving up and walking away from goals at the first thwarting of his efforts. Similarly, the person with access only to frustration and not to disappointment may find himself striving toward a goal that has long since proven unattainable, or at least not worth the effort it would take.

In fact, all emotions are worthwhile in some situation or another. When you become immobilized by an emotion you are either in a state that is inappropriate to your situation (such as feeling disappointed when you find that you can't play the violin after practicing for a week), or you do not have a way of moving from the emotion that you are feeling to others that are more appropriate (such as not being able to move from disappointment to frustration to determination when you discover that you can't yet play the violin).

Knowing the components of your emotional states will make it possible for you to understand why you respond in the ways you do. Furthermore, knowing the components of emotional states to which you presently do not have access will make it possible for you to create those emotions for yourself when you need and want them.

*Emotions Have Structure*

*Knowing Structure Leads to Appropriateness*

*Knowing Structure Allows You to Change Your Emotions*

*Knowing Structure Gives You Access to All Emotions*

The next chapter delivers the knowledge of structure that you need in order to avoid emotional traps and to build a life of emotional choice. Once you are familiar with the eight components that are the building blocks of emotions, you will have a basis for determining the best emotion for any situation. You will also know how to arrange those building blocks to construct the emotion you want. In the world of emotional choice, as in other worlds, knowledge is power. And knowledge of structure is the greatest power.

# *The Pieces of the Puzzle*

WEATHER IS PART OF OUR DAILY LIVES, AFFECTING US IN A hundred different ways. Although some people recognize weather as either great or lousy, most of us make many more distinctions about our daily climate, such as stormy, balmy, threatening, close, blistering, and fair. Each of these weather conditions is formed by the simultaneous occurrence of such factors as humidity, wind, temperature, cloud cover, air pressure, and terrain. The weather on any particular day is determined by how these factors interact. Similarly, when you cook, what you ultimately get to eat is determined by the interaction of ingredients, cooking time, temperature, and so on.

Like the weather and cooking, emotions are the manifestation of a set of factors or ingredients. Just as a thunderstorm is defined by particular qualities of humidity, wind, temperature, and cloud formation, and just as a pie crust is made by cooking certain ingredients in a certain combination at a certain temperature, so too are such emotions as anxiety and joy determined by a set of thinking patterns we call *components*. In fact, all emotions are determined by a set of components. Some of these components of emotions were introduced through examples in the previous chapters. In this chapter you will learn about these components explicitly and in detail. These components are, at present, probably unfamiliar to you as conscious distinctions, although they will certainly be familiar to you as personal experience. How, then, should we approach learning about them?

Learning to recognize the components that underlie emotions is much like learning to recognize the various tastes that blend to form the flavor of a wine. An ingenious and effective kit has been developed to teach anyone how to make such taste distinctions. The kit consists of four vials, each containing the unalloyed smell of one of the four essential components contributing to the taste of a wine. (The four components are the essences of fruit sugars, tannins, acid, and alcohol.) The idea is to become well enough acquainted with the smell and taste of each of these isolated components so that you can easily detect the various odors and tastes that have combined to make a particular wine.

Similarly, if you had never had the opportunity to hear individually the instruments that make up an orchestra, but had only heard full orchestras, it would be very difficult to pick out the separate sound of a single instrument. You may know the difference in sound between woodwinds and brass, but unless you have heard individually the timbres of an oboe, an English horn, and a bassoon, you probably would not be able to distinguish the contribution of each of these woodwind instruments to the total sound of the orchestra. Once you are familiar with them, however, you can both detect and better appreciate their role in producing the musical effects you are hearing.

The wine and orchestral examples we have just given illustrate one of the fundamentals of learning—the understanding that the whole is built out of knowledge of and appreciation for the parts. In order to appreciate and benefit from the material in the following chapters, you must be familiar with the distinctions with which we will be working. So we begin our exploration of the weather, tastes, and music of emotions by exploring first the components from which they are built.

**The Components of Emotions**

| | |
|---|---|
| *Time Frame* | *Comparison* |
| *Modality* | *Tempo* |
| *Involvement* | *Criteria* |
| *Intensity* | *Chunk Size* |

## Time Frame

For ten minutes Stephen, a member of our staff, had been trying to complete a conversation with his wife that should have taken only a few minutes. The bottleneck was their six-year-old son Jay, who was interrupting his parents every thirty seconds with questions, requests, and complaints. At first Stephen answered his son as briefly as possible so that he could get back to the conversation, but as the interruptions escalated, so did Stephen's temper. Inevitably, Jay made his last-straw interruption and Stephen felt himself coming unglued. As he glared down at the boy, eyes aflame, about to launch into a furious tirade, Stephen's imagination suddenly leapt to the future. In that future he saw his son full grown, acting rudely, and being isolated and unhappy as a result. At once the conversation of the moment seemed insignificant. The flame in Stephen's eyes died down to a glow. He knelt beside his son and began to explain to him what it means to be rude and what he needed to do to keep from being rude.

What made it possible for Jay to get a learning experience rather than a tongue lashing from his father? Stephen's initial feeling of irritation erupted into anger at having his present experience so badly marred by his son's behavior. The change in Stephen's response came when he shifted from his concern for the present (the conversation) to a future concern (Jay's happiness). Having made that shift in time frame, he considered Jay's present behavior from the perspective of an undesirable future, and so his emotions shifted from anger to concern and patience. When we speak of *time frames* we are speaking of the *past*, the *present*, and the *future*. Almost all emotions involve our referring to the past, present, or future. In fact, reference to a certain time frame is necessary in order for many emotions to exist at all.

As an example, consider something about which you feel apprehensive or anxious. If you attend to what is going on in your imagination you will notice that you are feeling that way about something that might happen in the future, whether imminent or remote. That is, feeling apprehensive or anxious involves imagining some unwanted *future* possibility. No matter how you search through your experience, you will not be able to find any examples of being apprehensive about something that has already happened or is actually happening now. In order to feel apprehensive now, you must refer to the time frame of the future.

By changing your attention to other time frames, you can create a contrast of emotions that will make it obvious that it is necessary to imagine unwanted future possibilities in order to generate feelings of apprehension or anxiety. A moment ago we asked you to think of something about which you feel apprehensive or anxious. Once steeped in those emotions, you can change your apprehension or anxiety to some other emotion simply by bringing your consciousness to the present, attending to such facts as where you are and what is going on around you now. Even when you are feeling apprehensive or anxious, the fact is that usually you are just fine *in the present*. We have found, typically, that you have to be fine in the present or your mind won't let you wander out into the future to generate anxiety. If you are not whole and safe right now, then your mind has much more pressing business to attend to in the present than considering unpleasant future possibilities.

As another example, regret is an emotion in which you are referring to the past—that is, considering how things *could have been* or what you *could have done* but didn't do. By shifting your attention to the future and considering what *could be* or what you *could do* you shift from regret into the emotion of, perhaps, hope. (Try it now with an example of your own.)

Similarly, in order to feel bored or restless you have to be attending to the time frame of the present—attending to what is *not* going on now. You can move from feeling bored and restless into feeling anticipation by shifting your attention from the present to something you are looking forward to in the not-too-distant future. The time frame to which an emotion refers may be significant in determining the qualities and impact of that emotion. And if you are experiencing an emotion for which time frame is an important component, then you can shift that emotion to another simply by shifting your attention to a different time frame.

## *Modality*

Ron, a member of one of our training groups, despairingly pronounced that "It is not possible to rid the world of hunger." While he agreed that it was possible for the Mets to win the World Series, a woman to become president, or a weatherman to be right about the weather, he sadly shook his head and insisted that ending world hunger was an impossibility. We asked him to imagine that the United Nations had decided to dole out problems to various citizens to solve, and that he had been selected as *the* person to tackle world hunger. He was reluctant to take on the assignment, but after he understood that he was the only one who could be given the responsibility for coming up with a plan, he accepted his charge. His immediate response was to start generating possible approaches, repeatedly using such hope-filled preambles as, "Well, we could . . .," "Perhaps if . . .," and "Possibly people could. . . ."

Like Ron's attitude regarding the possibility of ending world hunger, our beliefs about how necessary, how possible, how impossible, or how important things are can greatly affect our emotions—and vice versa. Believing that it is *necessary* for things to go smoothly has a very different impact on our responses than does believing that it is *possible* for things to go smoothly. Likewise, believing that it is *not possible* for things to go smoothly, or that it is *desirable* for things to go smoothly, have different impacts on us than do beliefs about necessity or possibility. When your subjective experience dictates that some particular thing is necessary, or possible, or impossible, or desirable, you are operating out of what we call a *modality*.

Some emotions are shaped by modalities to a greater degree than are others. Responsibility, for example, is an emotion that depends largely upon modalities for its qualities and effects. Perhaps you have been in a situation where something needed to be done, and, even though your skills were meager, you were the best-qualified person available to tackle the task. As a result, the task became yours to do. Thus challenged, you responded and behaved far above your known skill level. Your achievement in this case was a result of *feeling* responsible.

Believing that "it *needs* to be done" is expressing a modality of necessity. "It is mine to do" is also based upon the modality of necessity, conveying that it is necessary that *you* do it. Once you have accepted the fact that the task needs to be done, and is yours to do, you quit questioning whether or not you *can* do it and shift to considering *how* you can do it. When you feel responsible, "I must" is presupposed, and your thinking rallies to fulfill that presupposition.

A third component to feeling responsible is the question of whether or not you believe that you *can* do what needs to be done (a modality of *possibility*). How you answer this question largely determines how you will handle your responsibility. If you believe that you can't, or that it is not possible for you to do what needs to be done, then you will probably move to feeling inadequate or despairing and try to get out of doing what needs to be done. If instead you believe that you can measure up, then you will probably respond by feeling adequate or powerful and begin fulfilling your responsibility.

| | |
|---|---|
| ***"It needs to be done."*** | *There are consequences to doing or not doing it.* |
| ***"It is mine to do."*** | *I am the best qualified/most appropriate person to do it.* |
| ***"I can do it."*** | *I am able to do it now, or will be able to eventually.* |

You can test the necessity of each of these components for yourself by finding something you presently feel responsible to do, then eliminating in turn any one of those modality components. For instance, suppose that you feel responsible for improving the schools in your community. You could (just for a moment) believe that the schools are fine the way they are, or that no change in them would make a difference in the quality of the education their students receive (eliminating "needs to be done"). Or you could believe that enhancing schools is properly the job of teachers and administrators (eliminating "mine to do") . Or you could believe that there is nothing you can do about the schools (eliminating "can do it"). In each case, as soon as you eliminate or nullity one of those three components, the feeling of responsibility vanishes, to be replaced by something else.

So the result of believing that something needs to be done, that it is yours to do, and that you can do it, is a feeling of responsibility. Once you feel responsible for something, your thinking becomes oriented toward figuring out just how to fulfill that responsibility—that is, how to do what you need to do. The modality of impossibility shifts to one of possibility. This is precisely how Ron went from despair over the possibility of eliminating hunger on this planet to figuring out how to actually go about it.

Language is often a window to our thoughts, perceptions, and feelings; and a set of words describing modalities provides us with one of those windows. These words are merely verbal expressions of beliefs we have with regard to the necessity, possibility, and desirability of something. For instance, when we say that we "need to" or "must" do something we are expressing a modal belief of *necessity*. Words such as "could," "can," and "might" reflect a modal belief of *possibility*, while "can't" reflects a modal belief of *impossibility*. The belief that something is desirable or undesirable is communicated by such indicator words as "want," "will," "should," and "won't." Many of the emotions we all have are at least partly a function of the modalities we are using at the time. The following list contains some further examples.

| ***Indicator Words*** | ***Emotions*** |
|---|---|
| *Need* | Desperate, needy |
| *Must* | Pressured, overwhelmed, obsessed |
| *Should* | Obligated |
| *Should have/ shouldn't have* | Guilty, regretful |
| *Could* | Hopeful, optimistic, wary, cautious |
| *Can* | Able, adequate, confident, capable |
| *Might* | Vulnerable, apprehensive, curious |
| *Might have been/ could have been* | Disappointed |
| *Can't* | Helpless, inadequate |
| *Can't be done* | Despairing, resigned, hopeless |
| *Want* | Motivated, attracted, desirous, greedy, lustful |
| *Will* | Tenacious, determined, patient (when outcome is maintained), ambitious (for many people) |
| *Won't* | Stubborn |

Each of the indicator words given here represents a belief about the necessity, possibility, or desirability of something, and these modal beliefs contribute greatly to the creation of the emotions listed.

As with all of the distinctions presented in this chapter, modalities can be used to build wanted or needed emotions. Using "responsibility" as an example, you can bring yourself or someone else to feeling capably responsible by building in the necessary modality components of that emotion—that is, by effectively conveying to someone that:

- "It" needs to be done (in order to avoid negative consequences or to attain positive consequences);
- "It" is his to do (he is the best, only, or proper choice); and
- He can do "it" (what needs to be done is possible for him to do).

Remember, to get yourself or someone else to feel responsible in this way, it is important to know the reasons "it" needs to be done, and those reasons must be experienced as acceptable or worthy. It is not enough to make someone *be* responsible; that person must *feel* responsible if he is to wholeheartedly fulfill the task. For instance, few teenagers feel responsible for helping to babysit their little brothers and sisters. For them to feel responsible for babysitting their siblings, they first need to perceive it as important—for example, because it frees mom and dad to earn the money the family needs. The teenager then needs to accept the childcare as something that is his to do, either as a privilege, or as a job, or because there is simply no one else who can do it. And finally, the teenager must have a sense that he can do what needs to be done—that is, that he knows enough about taking care of little brother or sister to do it competently.

People whose feelings of responsibility are based on these three qualities are usually quite determined and in control of fulfilling their responsibilities. Simply saddling someone with a task, saying, in effect, "Here, you're supposed to do this," runs the risk of eliciting in him the modality of "I won't" or "I don't have to." You have then created in him a feeling of resistance, rather than of responsibility. And if such a person does accept the task as his to do, he may still believe that he can't do it, leaving him saddled with the responsibility yet feeling inadequate. The inclusion of the third step, the "I can," ensures that the feeling of responsibility also includes a sense of adequacy, forging the three steps into a single powerful force.

### *Involvement*

Ned, a cousin of Leslie's, had been out of high school for a year. He had no plans to go to college. In fact, he had no plans at all. He spent most of his days moping around the house, bleating out in every conversation things like, "I wish I had a job," "I'd sure like to have a car," and "I hope the guys call." During our yearly visit, we listened to about a day of Ned's hopes, then could listen no more. We looked Ned in the eye and asked, "Well, what in the hell are you going to *do* about it?" Ned stared back blankly. "Do?" he said. We spent the rest of the evening taking Ned through many different ways to go about getting a job. By the end of the evening, Ned saw his role in making some of his wishes come true, and the feelings of anticipation he experienced that evening were still with him when he went job hunting the next day.

Just as you can feel that something is possible or necessary or desirable, you can feel *actively* or *passively* involved. Ned had no feeling of direct and active involvement in making his wishes come true. There were forces moving around "out there" that would or would not grant him his wishes, so he felt that there was nothing for him to do in relation to his desires. (As soon as he decided that he wanted things to be different for himself, Ned created an *outcome*. The outcome is whatever change in emotion, behavior, or circumstance you want for yourself.)

Each of us has situations in which we feel actively engaged in the outcome, and other situations in which we feel only passively involved. Although Ned's feelings of passivity certainly resulted in passive behavior, we are not talking about active or passive *behavior* here, but of *feeling* that you are either instrumentally involved in shaping what occurs—"active"—or impotently subject to what occurs—"passive."

For instance, find something about which you feel ambitious, such as becoming a partner in your firm, getting the vegetable garden in, or arranging a nice evening with your mate, and then feel the ambition you have to make that outcome a reality. When you do this, you will notice that you feel a sense of active involvement in attaining your goal, a sense that there are things for you to *do*. If you take that sense of activeness away and replace it with a sense of waiting for events to fulfill your outcome, your feeling of ambition will vanish. For most people, feeling passive while maintaining the desired outcome creates the emotion of hope. The outcome is seen as something to wait for, something that is to come to you, rather than something you are going after. Conversely, substituting the feeling of active involvement in an outcome for which you are hoping will create ambition. Try each of these transformations with some of your own hopes and ambitions. In addition to an active involvement, you will discover that two of the components of ambition are a future time frame (thinking of a goal that resides in the near or distant future) and a modality of "I can and will." In fact, the future time frame and this modality contribute to the active involvement.

Feeling passive in relation to an outcome fosters an attitude of wait-and-see, as well as one of acceptance, however begrudging, of what circumstances offer you. Emotions that at least partly owe their qualities to this feeling of passivity include hope, apathy, complacence, satisfaction, loneliness, and calm. No matter how intensely you may hope for something, as long as it remains only a hope there is a feeling of having to wait and see whether or not you will get what you want. With complacence, satisfaction, and apathy, outcomes have been met, or perhaps do not exist, and you do not experience a need to do anything in relation to those outcomes. Feeling lonely involves wanting to be with people but feeling unable to do anything on your own initiative to make that outcome a reality.

As we mentioned earlier, feeling active engages in you a sense of purposeful involvement and personal ability to influence what is going on. Feeling actively engaged is part of what makes it possible to feel such emotions as determination, ambition, affection, curiosity, fear, disgust, and frustration. Each of these emotions is characterized by a pervading sense of needing to do something to fulfill some purpose: in the case of feeling determined, to get something done; in the case of feeling ambitious, to rise to a certain level; in the case of feeling curious, to figure something out; in the case of feeling frustrated, to make something turn out the way you want it to; and so on.

You are more likely to be passive if you have no outcome in mind in a given situation. If you do have an outcome in mind, you will be either active or passive in relation to attaining your outcome. Sometimes your outcome will involve going *toward* something (fostering a friendship, acquiring a new skill, feeling a certain way), while at other times your outcome will involve going *away* from something (getting rid of a headache, not repeating a mistake, avoiding a boorish person). The degree of involvement you feel and whether you are going toward or away from something combine to help create certain emotions. For example, emotions such as frustration, determination, ambition, aggression, affection, friendliness, and intrigue all involve a feeling of being active toward something. When you are frustrated you are feeling actively engaged in moving toward the attainment of something that has so far eluded you. Similarly, feeling aggressive, affectionate, or friendly involves feeling actively engaged in moving toward another person, and feeling intrigued involves feeling that you are actively moving toward finding out about something. Feeling passively involved *away* from an outcome is a key to such emotions as boredom, annoyance, loneliness, and self-pity, while feeling passively involved *toward* an outcome is an important part of forming such emotions as hope and patience.

## *Intensity*

Leslie glanced up from her magazine to check the time. She felt concerned about our son, Mark. It was a quarter past ten and he was still not home from the show. It was only fifteen minutes past the time Mark had promised to be home, but Leslie's mind was already straying to the consideration of some of the more unpleasant reasons why he might be late. When fifteen minutes later Mark still had not returned, Leslie began thinking about some of the *dire* possibilities, and soon her imagination had her feeling quite upset. As the minutes ticked by, Leslie began running the awful scenes in her head faster and faster, coming up with new twists, and adding more and more detail, until soon she was feeling quite anxious. She tossed her magazine aside and began pacing the room. As the awful images became more and more real, Leslie found herself peering out the window for approaching headlights and repeatedly glancing at the phone, willing it to ring. Unable to restrain herself any longer, she lunged for the telephone to call the police, the movie theater, Mark's friends, anyone! Then the front door opened.

Leslie's emotional journey from concern to hysterical desperation was powered almost solely by one component of her experience, that of *intensity*. Accompanying each emotional step she took was an increase in the intensity of the images she was making, including more images, enhanced detail, increased depth of colors, more accompanying sounds; an increase in the intensity of her movements, such as pacing the floor; and an increase in the intensity of the sensations she was feeling. As in the case of Leslie's emotional progression from concern to upset to anxiety to desperation, the distinct qualities of many emotions are due to their characteristic intensities. The intensity we are talking about here is not absolute, but subjective and relative. Although anger and disapproval are structurally very similar emotions, they are obviously of different intensities, anger being more intense than disapproval.

It is often possible to move from one emotion to another simply by changing the intensity of the experiences you are having at the time. For instance, find an example of some outcome that you recently attained about which you feel satisfied. When you are again feeling that satisfaction, increase the intensity of the emotion by making your internal images of what you did brighter and more colorful, making your feelings stronger, and changing your internal dialogue to include such praise as, "Wow, I did it, that's great! Look at all it does for me, and it means I'm such a great person!" For most people, increasing the intensity of feeling satisfied in this way takes them to feeling thrilled, or even ecstatic.

Of course, intensity is a continuum that covers not only more, but less as well. You can take the emotion of ecstasy and dull your images, sensations and feelings, and internal dialogue to the point that it becomes titillation or satisfaction. As straightforward and effective as changing intensity is, it rarely occurs to people to do it in order to have the kinds of emotional experiences they need or would like to have. For instance, if you take a moment to search through your own experiences you will probably find examples of situations in which you short-changed yourself by feeling only satisfied when you really deserved to feel ecstatic. Or there may have been times when you were thrilled or ecstatic when it would have been more appropriate to feel merely satisfied—for example, getting ecstatic over a dollar-an-hour raise, when what you actually needed and wanted was considerably more.

Examples of emotions that are structurally similar but which vary in their relative intensity include (from less to more intense):

*disappointed* ⟶ *sad* ⟶ *grieving*

*satisfied* ⟶ *happy* ⟶ *thrilled* ⟶ *ecstatic*

*concerned* ⟶ *upset* ⟶ *anxious* ⟶ *hysterical*

*curious* ⟶ *interested* ⟶ *aroused* ⟶ *lustful* ⟶ *obsessed*

*disapproving* ⟶ *angry* ⟶ *furious*

Although we show them going only in one direction, the arrows can go in both directions. If you need to, you can make your "lust" into the more tolerable "aroused," or your "anger" into the more tolerant "disapproval," by dulling the intensity of your sensations, images, and internal dialogue. However, reducing intensity can be like removing a spice from a soup. It's easy to add more, but difficult to take it out once it's in. Often it is easier to move from one of these emotions to another by changing other components rather than by reducing intensity. We'll go more deeply into that subject in a later chapter.

## *Comparison*

All of us have felt inadequate in certain situations at certain times, but Jonathan, a client of ours, was yoked to that emotion, feeling inadequate in virtually every situation, all of the time. He naturally shied away from setting goals for himself, and when he did he quickly succumbed to his ever-present feelings of inadequacy and gave up. Not surprisingly, he asked us to help him "stay interested in things" and to "stay with things until I get somewhere with them."

We soon discovered that Jonathan created the feeling of inadequacy in himself the same way that many of us do—that is, by making comparisons between himself and others. In making his comparisons he would "discover" what others can do or have done that he can't do or hasn't done. The other necessary ingredient was his belief that not being able to do what someone else can do meant that he was worth less than that other person. You can probably find your own examples of situations in which you compare yourself to others, come up lacking, and take that lack as proof that you have distasteful qualities. For instance, on the dance floor you see others as moving creatively and gracefully, while you see yourself as stumbling along with three left feet. That you do not move like the others on the dance floor means to you that you are not as good as the others, and so you feel inadequate.

Jonathan's comparisons were not limited to the dance floor, however. He constantly compared what he could do to the skills, talents, and accomplishments of other people. How others laughed, walked, ran, drove, smiled, talked, danced, socialized, made investments, and waited for elevators—literally everything was cause for comparison. Recognizing that Jonathan's penchant for comparison was completely habitual, we had him pay attention to the ways in which he was better now than in the past by having him constantly ask himself the question, "How have I improved?" Instead of trying to get him to stop making comparisons, we simply changed what he was comparing. He immediately went from feeling inadequate to feeling capable much more of the time and in many more situations. He also began behaving in accordance with that new emotional response by remaining interested and engaged in moving toward attaining what he wanted, rather than withdrawing as he had always done before.

As Jonathan demonstrated so well, we often pay attention to the degree to which things match or do not match one another. When you are attending only to how things *match*, what you tend to notice most are those things that seem to be the same as something you are holding as a standard. For instance, when you buy a new car suddenly you notice dozens of that same kind of car on the road every day. Out of all of the thousands of cars you pass, those that match yours stand out, as though last night everybody got the urge to buy the same car you did. Matching is an important component in creating the emotions of "agreeable" and "satisfied." An essential aspect of both of these emotions is that you are noticing the ways in which what you want has been or is being fulfilled.

When you want your son to do a good job on the lawn but notice only the edging he missed, ignoring the fact that the rest of the lawn looks great; or when your intimate evening with your lover is spoiled by the fact that your mate doesn't want to make love (even though he or she does feel like having a private, warm, and affectionate evening with you), you are *mismatching*. Mismatching is an important element in the emotions of disagreeable, frustrated, contemptuous, and disappointed.

Take the time now to reexperience your own personal examples of feeling any of these four emotions and you will notice that you are attending to what you have gotten or have done that does *not match* what you had wanted or intended. Now take some of those same examples and search for ways in which what you got or did *matched* at least a small portion of what you had wanted, and observe how your feelings change. For many people, mismatching also underlies feeling humorous, finding unexpected or bizarre discrepancies amusing.

When you attend to the *degree* to which things are the same or different you are doing what Jonathan does—that is, making comparisons. When making comparisons, you are noticing whether you are more or less graceful than another person, more or less intelligent than your sister, more or less affluent than your neighbor (or than you were last year), and so on. As Jonathan demonstrated, making comparisons between your abilities and accomplishments and those of other people can form the basis for feeling inadequate. Such comparisons can also underlie feeling smug, contemptuous, or envious, as when you compare what another person has to what you have.

Although comparisons commonly underlie these emotions, they may be generated by mismatching as well. Thus you can envy your neighbor because of her new car, or feel inadequate when your peers have attained job security and you have not. In fact, all of the emotions listed above as being partly based upon mismatching may also be generated by making comparisons. You may feel disappointed if a movie you are watching is less captivating than you had expected, or feel frustrated with your progress on a project that seems to have no end. Both mismatching and comparisons can provide you with an awareness of *difference*—either absolute, in the case of matching, or relative, in the case of comparisons. It is this recognition of difference that is so important to creating the emotions listed above for both mismatching and comparisons.

## *Tempo*

Our son Mark knew that he didn't have the greatest serve in tennis, but he also knew that he played far better than he had been demonstrating in the match so far. He had double-faulted several times now, and each time it happened he felt more frustrated. As Mark's frustration grew, so did his number of errors. Soon he was muttering to himself in an angry staccato voice and pacing about rapidly, his eyes alternately focusing with searing intensity and flitting about the court in an effort to take everything in as quickly as possible. When it was Mark's turn to serve again he stepped to the line and tossed the ball up. But when it went sailing into the air far too high to be well hit, he stopped himself, saying, "Wait a minute. I've got to slow down." He bounced the ball slowly and steadily on the court for a few moments, slowing down all his movements, right through to his serve. The serve was much better. Between plays, Mark continued operating at a slower pace, and soon he was no longer feeling frustrated, but determined to get his game back to what he knew it could be.

Sometimes we feel that we are moving quickly, sometimes slowly, sometimes steadily, or erratically, and so on. In other words, there is a tempo to our experiences. *Tempo* is one of those qualities of experience that is rarely recognized, yet it is almost always a compelling aspect of our ongoing experience. The most explicit and familiar use of tempo is in movies and television, where background music is frequently used to help create in the audience the emotional responses that the filmmaker intends to evoke. Watch a movie with the sound off for awhile, then turn the sound on but don't watch it, and you will quickly get a direct experience of the importance music tempo plays in creating your experience. When we listen to music, we sometimes match the tempos of our selections to the tempos we are feeling, and at other times select music built upon tempos that we would like to be feeling—for example, putting on a vibrant, lively piece to counteract a feeling of inertia.

Tempo seems to pervade all of our emotions. Emotions that rely upon fast tempos include excited, panicky, restless, impatient, anxious, and angry. Slow tempos underlie the emotions of bored, lonely, apathetic, discouraged, patient, accepting, and satisfied. Feeling anxious or nervous usually involves fast but uneven tempos, while a slow, even tempo helps to create the feeling of calm.

When we say that these emotions "rely" upon certain tempo patterns, we mean that those tempo patterns are significant in determining the subjective quality of the emotions. When we feel excited, the tempo we feel is *fast*. In fact, sometimes we feel *so* excited that our tempo speeds up to the point of missing much of what is going on around us. At that point we are "moving" so fast that we allow no time for input. Even if you are not zooming along at such a frenetic rate, it is nevertheless virtually impossible to feel excited and to experience a slow tempo at the same time. (Try it.)

In the other direction, feeling patient involves maintaining a *slow* tempo. It is impossible to feel patient and experience a fast tempo at the same time. (Again, try it.) In fact, the most common response that people have when they realize that they are feeling inappropriately *im*patient is to take a slow, deep breath and exhale fully, which has the immediate effect of slowing down one's tempo and frequently leads to a feeling of increased patience. Both patience and impatience involve having a clearly defined future outcome. The significant difference between them is that patience involves a slow tempo, while impatience involves a fast tempo. (Patience also has a longer time frame; its outcome is likely to be further in the future.) You can explore this difference yourself by bringing to mind something about which you are feeling impatient, then slowing down your tempo; and by bringing to mind something about which you are feeling patient, then speeding up your tempo.

As we saw in the above examples, changing your tempo can dramatically change your emotions. For instance, the tempo of feeling discouraged is relatively slow. When you speed up the tempo of discouragement, however, it often turns into frustration, which is a more useful emotion if you want to continue to be engaged in attaining your desired outcome. Going in the other direction, when you are excited about something in the present and slow down the tempo, the feeling usually shifts to something like happy or contented, emotions which some people enjoy more than feeling excited.

The best emotion for you to have in a particular situation depends upon that situation and what you want your experience to be in it. Slow down the tempo you are experiencing while feeling anxious and the emotion will probably go to dread, which may be a better choice for you if it is not as incapacitating as anxiety. Speed up the tempo of bored and it goes to restless, which may be useful in helping to propel you from a boring situation, but may also be useless and unpleasant if it is a situation about which you have little choice, such as waiting in line or crawling along in bumper-to-bumper traffic. In situations like these, it would be better to change your emotion by changing time frames. Why not recall a touching memory and feel nostalgia? Or perhaps it would be more enjoyable for you to think of a vacation, an accomplishment, or a romantic interlude that is in your future so that you can feel pleasurable anticipation.

## *Criteria*

The steady hand with which our friend Katy had answered the telephone was shaking when she dropped the receiver back into its cradle a few minutes later. When her secretary asked what was the matter, Katy explained that the boss wanted her to report at the next meeting on one of the big accounts she was developing. Katy's secretary tried to reassure her, saying, "You've been on that account for a year now. You know it backward and forward." Katy collapsed back into her chair muttering, "Forget it. The meeting's been pushed up to tomorrow. There's no way I can have all that material down pat." For the next three hours Katy worked on her presentation, but she knew that she would need at least a week to prepare adequately. As the hours passed, her anxiety grew. She became so panic-stricken, in fact, that she was on the verge of taking a tranquilizer to calm herself down, when the telephone rang again. The hand that set the receiver down this time was rock steady. It had been her boss again, this time apologizing because he had been called away and would not be there for her presentation. Katy smiled at her secretary. "With just the department heads there, I only need the highlights. Tomorrow will be a piece of cake," she said languidly.

It may have occurred to you that, of course, you do not just throw together any old time frame, modality, intensity, tempo, etc., and get an emotion. Emotions always occur within a particular context or situation—although you may be unaware of the context, as when you feel anxious but have not recognized that your anxiety relates to an upcoming presentation you must give. Situations change; and when they do, what is important to you changes as well. For instance, when she thought her boss was going to be present for her report, it was important to Katy that she have her material "down pat," and she felt anxious. But when she found out that her boss would *not* be there, it became important only to be able to "hit the highlights," and she felt confident. The term we use to refer to those things that you think are important is *criteria.*

Criteria are the standards that you are applying in a certain situation. In Katy's case, the criterion that she initially applied to her presentation was that of having it "down pat." That criterion and what she believed to be her actual level of preparedness combined to make her feel anxious. If she had thought that she did have it down pat then she would have felt excited or confident, rather than anxious. When her boss's absence made it possible for Katy to change her criterion to having her presentation "hit the highlights," her emotional response to the presentation changed as well.

As we have shown in many examples in this chapter, when you change a significant component your emotional experience also changes. In this example of anxiety, if the modality had been changed from *necessity* to *possibility*, and involvement from *passive* to *active*, Katy would have felt challenged rather than anxious. Similarly, if you change the criteria you are using, while leaving all of the other components intact, your emotional response will change as well. Like the other components we have described, criteria interacts simultaneously with all of the other components to create your emotions at any given moment.

Some specific examples will make the effect of criteria clearer. Let's say a friend of yours is viewing his current situation through a set of components that includes a *future* time frame orientation, a modality of *necessity* ("It will happen"), a *passive* sense of involvement, and a *high* level of intensity. Now suppose that he has just found out that his wife is pregnant. Using the components just described, how will he feel? The answer is, we can't tell until we know what criteria he is using. If he is using the criterion of *gaining something* (that is, he is perceiving the pregnancy in relation to what he is gaining), then he will feel something like pleasurable anticipation or excitement. However, if that person, using those same components, uses the criterion of *losing something,* he might feel dread at the loss of freedom the child will mean. All that has changed is the criterion which, in the first example, is *gaining something,* and in the second, *losing something.*

***Going to be a father***

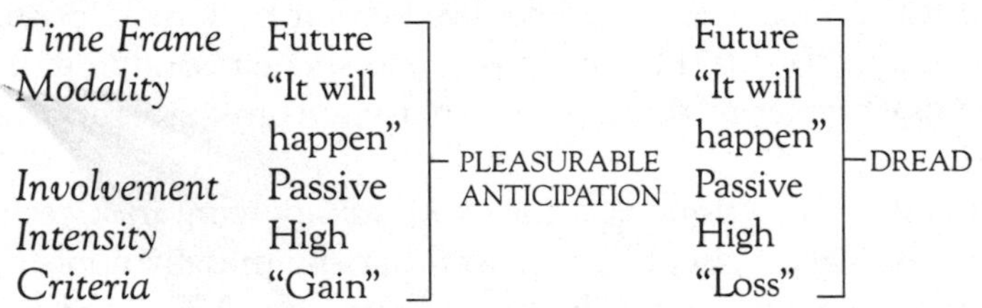

| | | | | |
|---|---|---|---|---|
| *Time Frame* | Future | | Future | |
| *Modality* | "It will happen" | | "It will happen" | |
| *Involvement* | Passive | PLEASURABLE ANTICIPATION | Passive | DREAD |
| *Intensity* | High | | High | |
| *Criteria* | "Gain" | | "Loss" | |

As another example, let's suppose that when his boss includes him in a business lunch for the first time, a person is operating out of the *present,* modality of *possibility* ("could be"), *active* involvement, *comparing, high* intensity, and the criterion of "acceptance" (that is, being accepted is important). This person would probably feel grateful or relieved. Using the same components and the same situation, but changing the criterion to "What can I get out of this?" this person might feel eager or ambitious.

***Asked to lunch by the boss for the first time***

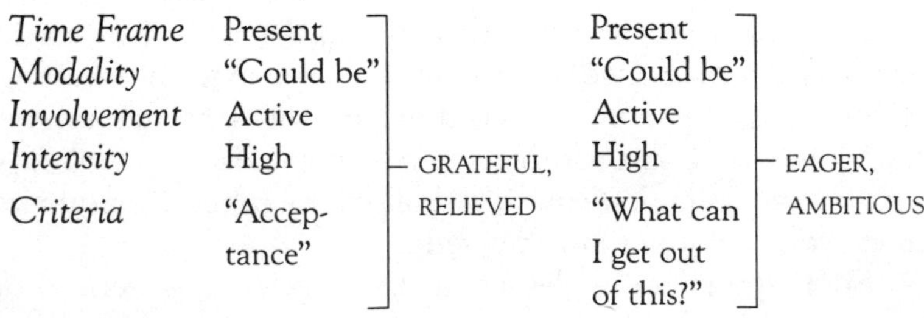

| | | | | |
|---|---|---|---|---|
| *Time Frame* | Present | | Present | |
| *Modality* | "Could be" | | "Could be" | |
| *Involvement* | Active | | Active | |
| *Intensity* | High | GRATEFUL, RELIEVED | High | EAGER, AMBITIOUS |
| *Criteria* | "Acceptance" | | "What can I get out of this?" | |

Like tempo, time frame, modality, involvement, intensity, and matching/mismatching/comparing, criteria are elements of your emotional experience that provide ways of dramatically influencing the quality of your experience.

## *Chunk Size*

It is likely that when Katy thought about her presentation she was thinking in terms of the entire task. Her feelings probably would have been different if she had instead broken it down into much smaller pieces. For instance, instead of working at the daunting task of putting together THE PRESENTATION, she could have worked one at a time on the less forbidding tasks of assembling the relevant information, deciding what her audience needed to hear, outlining a presentation sequence, designing visual aids, and memorizing important facts. Of course, Katy probably took all of these preparatory steps. The difference is in how she thinks about the presentation. Is it one large task, or a group of small tasks? It can be perceived either way, but the emotional impact of these two ways is quite different.

Frances' bank had failed to credit her account with a large deposit she had made to cover her taxes, leaving her account in the red and her checks bouncing all over town. Although terrified of confronting the sanctimonious stonefaces at the bank, she had nevertheless gone there to demand that they immediately reinstate her funds. In this she had failed, and now she was back home, feeling angry with the bank and utterly dissatisfied with herself. When Frances explained to her consoling friend that she felt angry because of the bank's lack of regard and dissatisfied because she had not gotten the outcome she had intended, her friend suggested, "Well, at least you did your best." Frances shook her head and said, "No I didn't." Going for something a little less ambitious, her friend said, "Well, at least you made an effort." Frances snorted, "Some effort." In a last-ditch effort, her friend pleaded, "You must have accomplished something!" Frances reflected for a moment then, laughing, recalled, "True. Even though I was scared, I told them, 'You haven't heard the last of me,' and walked out." Frances snapped her fingers, "Just like that." Her friend looked a little skeptical and snapped her fingers the way Frances had done. Frances nodded and repeated, "Just like that." And she felt satisfied that she had at least expressed her anger.

It had been important to Frances that she adequately confront the monolithic bank; her criterion, then, was *adequacy.* When she first looked at how she had handled the situation all she could see was that she had not acted in a way that she considered adequate, and so she felt dissatisfied. What moved Frances from feeling dissatisfied to feeling satisfied was that she finally focused her attention on a portion of her performance that she *did* consider adequate. Telling the banker, "You haven't heard the last of me," and walking out, was a relatively small portion of the overall outcome of getting the bank to reinstate her funds. In our parlance, the overall outcome represents a relatively "large chunk," while warning the banker and walking out is a relatively "small chunk."

*Chunk size* is a description of how much you are attending to in your experience out of what it is possible to attend to in a particular situation. Each time Frances' friend tried to make her feel better she was, in effect, suggesting that Frances "chunk down" her experience and pay attention to smaller and smaller portions of it. "Doing your best" is of a relatively smaller chunk size than is "attaining your outcome," while "You made an effort" suggested that Frances consider her adequacy in handling an even smaller portion of the confrontation. Making an effort is only a part of doing one's best. Telling the banker, "You haven't heard the last of me" is an even smaller chunk in that it was only a part of what went into "making an effort," the part concerning expressing her anger. In each instance, Frances was considering smaller and smaller ways in which she had behaved adequately when demanding that the bank return her money.

As suggested in the example above, chunking down leads you to attend to smaller and smaller details, while chunking up takes you to a broader, more inclusive picture. For instance, suppose that you are thinking of starting a garden. If you chunk down what is involved in having a garden you will begin considering such things as what to plant, how to prepare the soil, how to schedule time for working on the garden, and so on. These are some of the pieces (small chunk outcomes) that combine to create the larger outcome of having a garden. Chunking up from "having a garden" might take you to the even larger outcome of "feeling productive." In other words, having a garden might be one of the underlying elements in creating the larger outcome of feeling productive.

Chunk size is one of the ways in which we can change our emotions. Frances was able to feel satisfaction by chunking down her experience to a level at which she considered that she had satisfied her criterion of performing adequately. People often feel incapable when they view a task at a vast chunk size that includes outcomes they think are beyond their abilities. When people chunk down such formidable tasks into the various steps and skills needed to attain the outcome, their emotion usually shifts to feeling capable. You can try this yourself by finding an example of some goal you want to achieve, but which you feel incapable of achieving. Start chunking it down into smaller and smaller pieces until you get it down to those pieces of behavior, perception, skills, or abilities that you consider to be within your grasp. Organize your approach one step at a time. Your emotion will change.

We do not mean to imply that you should reduce all of your experience down to small chunk sizes. There is nothing inherently right or wrong about any chunk size. Large-chunk perceptions can lead you to some wonderful experiences as well.

> On the first and second day of the flight, we were all noticing our countries, saying, "That's my home," Prince Sultan ibn Salman al Saud of Saudi Arabia, who rode on the shuttle Discovery last June with French and American crewmates, said in Dallas. "By the third day, you only see continents. By the fifth day, you see only the Earth—it becomes one place, your home. . . . It's an amazing feeling. [Los Angeles *Times*, September 15, 1985]

Some emotional states are characterized by certain chunk sizes. For example, awe, wonder, overwhelmed, and discouraged almost always involve attending to things at a relatively large chunk size. You may feel awe when looking at something as big as the Grand Canyon or something as small as a spider web, but in both instances you will find that you are attending to the *whole*. As soon as you start taking apart the Grand Canyon (into its various levels, branching canyons, bands of color) or the spider web (into the patterns of the strands, the foundation construction, places where it glistens), you will discover that the feeling of awe slips away, replaced perhaps by feelings of fascination, curiosity, or appreciation.

Emotions that characteristically involve relatively small chunk sizes include irritation and disagreeableness. In general, when you are feeling irritated you are attending to all of the little things that someone is doing that you don't like. For instance, you might find your child's penchant for interrupting your conversations irritating. If, however, you were attending to your child's behavior in relation to a larger chunk size ("What does my child need?"), you would probably have a very different emotional response to the interruption—perhaps feeling curious, patient, or concerned. Likewise, feeling disagreeable invariably involves responding to relatively small chunks of information, with the emotion turning into such feelings as philosophical, outraged, or tolerant when considering the same situation at a relatively large chunk size. (Remember, there is a difference between being irritable and feeling irritated, and between being disagreeable and feeling disagreeable. You can, for instance, *feel* sympathetic and yet *behave* in a disagreeable way.)

Relatively few emotions are necessarily based upon one particular chunk size. Although most emotions are qualitatively affected by the chunk size you are using at the time, the important consideration is, What is a *useful* chunk size? What is the appropriate amount of detail for *you* in this situation? For instance, suppose Don feels confident with regard to his ability to handle the various tasks involved in fulfilling the larger outcome of starting a new business. But when he regards the outcome at the relatively larger chunk size of "starting a new business," his feeling of confidence wavers, perhaps disappearing altogether to be replaced by feeling daunted or hopeless. In this case, it is more useful for Don to chunk at the level of "underlying tasks" than at the level of "whole outcome."

However, there is nothing about chunking small that necessarily leads to feeling confident. Unlike Don, Sue feels most confident when she considers accomplishing the whole outcome, and often feels confused and overwhelmed with details when she chunks down to consider the various tasks that attaining that outcome will require of her. For Sue to feel confident, chunking large is more useful than chunking small. The appropriateness of a particular chunk size, then, depends largely upon the person using it, the situation that person is in, and the emotion that is needed or wanted. You need to experiment to discover the best chunk size for you to use in the various situations in which you find yourself. Emotions for which it is particularly important that you not be confined to one chunk size, but have the ability to shift from one size to another, include satisfied, capable, appreciative, and understanding.*

## *Some In-Depth Examples*

In this chapter we have discussed the major components that are significant in creating your emotions: Time Frame, Modality, Involvement, Intensity, Comparison, Tempo, Criteria, and Chunk Size. There are others that we have not included because they are relatively insignificant in terms of actually determining what you feel. If you become familiar with the eight components just described, you will have what you need to be able to choose and change your emotions and thereby choose and change the quality of your ongoing experience. As we have illustrated, changing one of the significant components will change your emotion. Your emotions are yours to choose and enjoy, not simply to react to and endure.

*Significant components* are those that, when altered, do change your emotion, evolving it into some other emotion or simply dissipating it. For example, all of your emotions have tempo qualities (along with time frame, modality, intensity, etc.), but tempo may not be *the* significant component for a particular emotion of yours. That is, you may be able to change the tempo you feel and yet the emotion remains relatively unchanged. To give you a better understanding of how these components interact with one another to create emotions, here are a couple of in-depth examples of contrasting emotions.

### *Lethargic vs. Curious*

Some otherwise ambitious and energetic people become indifferent and lazy when faced with the chore of cleaning out old files, or the basement, garage, or closet. The files are overflowing, you can't get the car into the garage without knocking over sacks full of aluminum cans and stacks of newspapers and old bicycles, and

*You can find out a great deal more about both chunk size (under the name "relative specificity") and criteria in *The EMPRINT Method: A Guide to Reproducing Competence*, by Cameron-Bandler, Gordon, and Lebeau.

the closet is a deathtrap waiting to crush the next unsuspecting person who opens its door. You know that these things need attention . . . but you just can't bring yourself to tackle them. The emotion that people most commonly feel when they can think of things to do yet lack the will or motivation to act is "lethargy." Feeling lethargic is based upon the ambivalence you experience toward tasks that you believe you should do but that you don't want to do. Another common example is the feeling of lethargy that steals over many people when they think about sorting through last year's check stubs, receipts, and records in order to prepare their taxes.

Typically, the tempo of lethargy is slow. Your senses seem dulled and your responses to what goes on around you slacken. One of our clients likened the sensation to swimming in peanut butter. When you are feeling lethargic, sounds may also seem slowed, muffled, and dulled. Your body feels heavy, and your attention wanders. This dulling of, and removal from, the present makes sense because, typically, people feel lethargic about some present task, rather than a past activity or future endeavor.

| | | |
|---|---|---|
| *Time Frame* | Present | |
| *Modality* | "I should/need to, but don't want to" | LETHARGY |
| *Involvement* | Passive | |
| *Tempo* | Slow | |

"Curious," on the other hand, is the emotion that people usually feel when they are facing a puzzle or question to which they want an answer. You may feel curiosity when you find a slip in your mailbox informing you of a package waiting for you at the post office; or when you discover an interesting and unfamiliar plant growing in your garden; or when the caller hangs up just as you answer the telephone; or when a baby is on the way and you can't wait to find out whether it will be a boy or a girl. In each case the situation is the same. That is, something has raised a question in your mind that you want answered.

The tempo of feeling curious is certainly accelerated compared to that of feeling lethargic. The body feels lighter, the senses become sharper and more alert, and attention is focused on anything that might contain the answer to the question being asked. Also, when you are feeling curious your internal dialogue is generally filled with questions and sometimes speculative answers to those questions. (Where is it? What is it? How does it work? What's going to happen? Will this do it? Does it need a little more? What will happen if I just give this a little twist?)

Whatever the questions that initiate and sustain the feeling of curiosity, your attention is focused upon some potential source of answers. This source of answers may be within yourself, as when you try to figure out who might have been calling you, or in the outside world, as when you give "it" a little twist to find out what happens. In either case, you are *open to input*. This openness is the result of certain criteria, such as that it is important to understand, or to appreciate, or to know. When you are curious you are very receptive to input, whether it is in the form of perceptual stimuli, ideas, or the opinions of others. If we put curious, skeptical, and suspicious on a scale of subjective receptivity, we find "curious" to be the most open of the three. (In fact, when one is curious, one often readily accepts at face value what is being offered.) Skeptical, on the other hand, includes a search for the flaw in what is being offered, while suspicious is based upon a belief (and criterion) that there is foul play to be identified, and is therefore the least open of the three. In a learning situation, a mixture of curiosity and skepticism is most useful.

Unlike lethargy, curiosity has the power to propel us to take action. Have you ever suddenly remembered some item that you owned but had not seen in years, and then begun to wonder where it was? As you speculated on its whereabouts your curiosity grew until you found yourself rummaging through your desk, closets, and garage looking for it. As your speculation about where that item might be changed into a decision to find it, your curiosity may have evolved into a feeling of determination.

Here's another example of the power of curiosity. Somewhere on a later page of this chapter, embedded in the type itself, is a pictogram of something. Can you identify it?

Having read the above, are you curious enough to thumb through the remaining pages to find the embedded drawing? Do you want to discover it for yourself?

Like the questions posed above, the easiest means of creating curiosity in yourself is to ask questions about an aspect of something you are already at least mildly interested in. The effect of such questions is enhanced if they are about something that is of personal significance. For instance, a dedicated teacher may feel curious when he starts asking himself questions about how soap works, but he will almost certainly feel much more curious when he considers questions about what makes it possible for people to learn. A chemist, on the other hand, may find herself more intensely curious about the properties of soap than about those of learning.

Curiosity is an excellent emotion to use to initiate behavior. This is because of the fact that for most people curiosity easily evolves into feeling motivated and determined. This evolution is usually the result of the answers you are seeking moving from something you *want* to know (modality of possibility) to something you feel you *must* know (modality of necessity). If instead you increase the tempo you are feeling while you are curious, then your emotions may shift to restless or impatient—you must have the answer *now.*

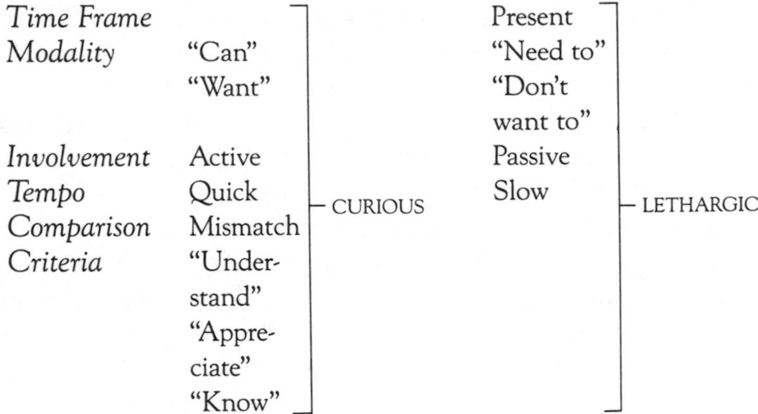


Notice that modality, involvement, and tempo are the only components that are significant for both feeling curious and feeling lethargic. Even though the actual modality, level of involvement, and pace may be different for each emotion, it is important to realize that these components are shared by each. Because they are significant to both, changing one or more of these three components can be your ticket out of lethargy. They are your transportation to curiosity and points beyond.

To feel curious you need to have a sense of being actively involved, you need to be using a criterion of wanting to know or understand, and you need to notice mismatches between what you know and what you are observing. The other components can be almost anything and still leave you feeling curious. You can feel curious in relation to the past, present, or future; you can feel that you must understand, could understand, or want to understand; your feeling of curiosity may be intense or mild; your tempo may be fast, making you impatiently curious, or slow, making you patiently curious; the chunk size you are curious about may be minute or immense, and it may diminish or increase as you learn more about the subject.

To feel lethargic you need to be considering in the present something that you must or should do *and* that you do not want to do (time frame and modalities); you need to have little sense of involvement with the outcome; and your tempo needs to be quite slow. The other components are insignificant to feeling lethargic. For instance, you might feel intensely lethargic or only mildly lethargic; you could be noticing how what is going on around you matches, mismatches, or compares with other things; and you could be using a wide range of criteria, such as time, interest, effort, rewarding, career advancement, and so on.

These descriptions are the components of subjective experience you need to change in yourself in order to move from one emotion to another. When you are feeling lethargic you probably won't be getting much done. That is the behavioral effect of lethargy. Certainly there are times when that is not a problem. But most of the time when you are feeling lethargic, you really wish that you were getting things done. So most of the time you probably either wait until your mood changes, allowing you to get on with the task, or you force yourself to get on with it while continuing to feel lethargic, but now overlaid with emotional tones of resentment and anger.

Wouldn't it be better to be able to change your feelings so that they were in accord with doing the task at hand? A first step in that direction might be to begin asking yourself questions about the task, questions to which you don't know the answers. Ideally, those questions should touch upon areas of personal importance or interest. For example, if you are getting your tax materials together, you might wonder how long-term tax planning could affect the security of your family. If you increase your tempo at the same time, you will find yourself feeling curious, which is a much more useful and flexible emotion than lethargic when it comes to getting things done.

Suppose that you have gotten yourself to feeling curious, but that you are still not compelled to get out of your chair and roll up your sleeves. What you need then is the motivation and determination that underlie making the necessary effort. You need to change the things you *want* to know about into things that you *need* or *must* know about. The result will be a feeling of motivation and determination that is likely to propel you into action. And if, in this pursuit, you discover that you are feeling restless or impatient and you don't want to feel that way, you know that you need to slow down your tempo in order to return you to the emotional levels of curiosity and determination.

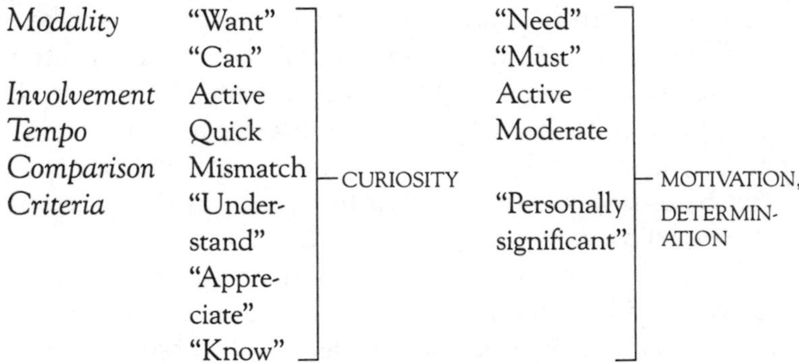


Again, you *do* have choices about your own emotions once you know how to affect your experience. And through your emotions you can dramatically affect your behavior as well, as in the previous example when you went from doing nothing to being actively engaged. Do you ever find yourself in a situation in which you would like to feel curious but do not? How might you be able to affect your experience the next time you are in such a situation so that you *do* feel curious? Or even determined? Are you curious *now* about the answers to these questions?

## *Overwhelmed vs. Motivated*

All of us have felt overwhelmed at one time or another. Say you are cooking a meal for company, the kids are arguing, the telephone is ringing every five minutes, you're not dressed yet, and your guests have just driven up. Or your stack of work just got doubled, you have a dozen phone calls to return within the hour, and each phone call results in even more work. Whatever the actual situation may be, your mind is filled with undone tasks, all of which seem in urgent need of attention. In short, you feel overwhelmed.

Feeling overwhelmed is the result of a couple of factors operating together. For one thing, you are keeping in mind at the same time *all* of the things you have to do. Obviously, for most of us, at any given moment there are a number of things that we could or should be doing. However, sometimes we hold constant in our consciousness just one or two of those tasks, while at other times we are conscious of *all* of those possible tasks. When we do that, we are well on the way to feeling overwhelmed.

The other ingredient that is needed to feel overwhelmed is a sense of urgency about completing those tasks. That is, a modality of necessity is attached to the tasks, making them things that "must," "have to," or "need to" be done to prevent some negative consequences from happening (people feeling let down, project ruined, loss of respect, etc.). This sense of urgency makes you hold your breath, increases the tension in your body, and fills your internal dialogue with incomplete questions and statements as your attention flits from one to another of the many necessary tasks you are facing.

But the primary property of feeling overwhelmed is the first one we discussed—that you are *simultaneously* keeping in mind a whole slew of things that *must* be done. Because the tasks are kept as a mob, you don't set priorities on them or put them in a sequence, which would allow you to temporarily set some of them aside in favor of others that you have designated as "more important" or "first." As long as the tasks are kept in mind simultaneously, there is more to do than can be done in the perceived time available. If your feeling of being overwhelmed persists, it may even evolve into feeling immobilized or hopeless.

There are some important differences between feeling overwhelmed and feeling motivated. When you are feeling motivated, typically you are imagining an outcome that you find attractive. In fact, the primary characteristic of motivation is attraction. Motivation contains an "I want" (modality of desire), along with some idea of what is desired. Usually an "I can get it" (modality of possibility) is perceived as well.

The tempo of feeling motivated is not as frenetic as that of feeling overwhelmed, but it nevertheless may be experienced as relatively fast. When feeling motivated you are also oriented toward the future. Specifically, there is something that you desire and could possibly attain in the future. That future may be either close at hand or far down the road. For instance, you may feel motivated to resolve an argument in which you are embroiled with your mate, to get a snack, to finish updating your résumé for a job interview tomorrow morning, or to take care of your financial security for your old age.

Also, when you feel motivated there is something that you don't have yet—and that "something" is either going to be fun or valuable, or both. You are making a comparison between what you have now and what you could or will attain in the future. This comparison results in your paying attention to how you will be better off in the future than you are in the present. More often than not, what people want is a certain experience, which they believe will result from doing or having whatever it is that they are holding as their desired outcome.

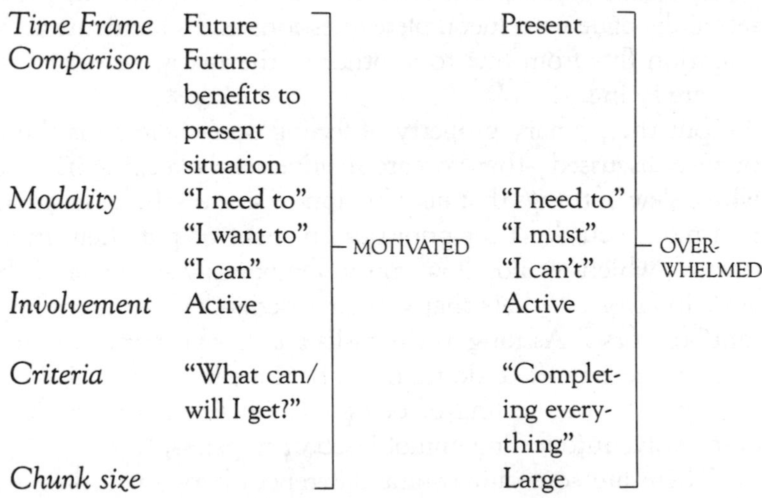

| | MOTIVATED | OVERWHELMED |
|---|---|---|
| *Time Frame* | Future | Present |
| *Comparison* | Future benefits to present situation | |
| *Modality* | "I need to"<br>"I want to"<br>"I can" | "I need to"<br>"I must"<br>"I can't" |
| *Involvement* | Active | Active |
| *Criteria* | "What can/will I get?" | "Completing everything" |
| *Chunk size* | | Large |

It's important to understand the structure of motivation. Certainly, the usefulness of feeling motivated has long been appreciated—witness the wealth of books, seminars, tapes, television shows, and training programs intended to teach you how to motivate yourself or others. The most successful of these manage, even if inadvertently, to build in the experiential pieces underlying the feeling of motivation—the pieces described above.

Obviously it's more useful to you to generate your own motivation than to rely on a tape or a training program. You can do this by discovering what in your world *naturally* leads you to want to engage in a given activity. To discover this, identify some activities that you already are genuinely motivated to do. Once you have found several, look at them in terms of their common elements. For instance: Are all these activities self-initiated? Or are they all undertaken at the request of others? Are they activities that you are good at? That you consider useful? Do they involve interacting with other people, or are they primarily solitary pursuits? Do they have open time frames (that is, to be attained whenever they are attained), or does each one have a definite deadline? Is there a specified reward for attaining the outcome? How do you feel about yourself as a result of doing each of them?

Once you have identified the components that result in your feeling motivated to do something, you can begin to orchestrate your perceptions about other, currently unattractive activities so that they become objects of motivation as well. You will know what qualities you need to infuse into a task or outcome in order to respond to it with a feeling of motivation. If some task is currently unattractive, but you would like to feel motivated to pursue it, you have only to reorient that task so that it fulfills your motivational needs.

For instance, suppose that activities you have felt motivated to pursue in the past include planting a vegetable garden, writing books, and taking your children to zoos and museums. Reviewing these examples, you discover that to be motivated, in each case you needed to believe that what you were doing would benefit others, that doing it would teach you something, and that it would be fun. Now you know the characteristics of activities that are, for you, naturally motivating.

Suppose, then, you are faced with the need to manage your money—something that you wish you were motivated to tackle. Knowing what you now know about what motivates you, you need only to discover the ways in which learning to manage your money will fulfill your requirements for motivation. You might determine that managing your money will help protect and provide for your spouse and children, that it will teach you something about economics, and that making and juggling investments will be fun for you in the same way that researching and outlining a book is fun. Once you have infused money management with these qualities, it will naturally become a source of motivation.

## *What You Have Now*

Throughout this chapter we have emphasized the fact that your emotions are the manifestation of certain perceptual components, and that if you change those components your emotions will change. The set of distinctions presented in this chapter provides you with a way of describing any emotion in terms of the significant components that go into creating them. Once you understand the structure of an emotion, you can also understand how it has the effect that it does upon your experience and your behavior. Once you know the significant components involved in creating an emotion of yours, it becomes possible for you to change that emotion to one that is more satisfying or appropriate for the situation you happen to be in.

Knowing the structure of your emotions can become the basis for building a personal world for yourself that offers you the freedom and power to direct your own emotional experience along those paths that preserve your well-being and lead you toward fully being and expressing who you are. Leslie and I have built such a world for ourselves. We used our knowledge of the structure of emotions to create the freedom and power we now enjoy, and we have learned how to sustain our free and empowering world by utilizing the components of emotions—at every opportunity, every day.

We both change our emotions by changing time frames, and we often do it in different ways. Leslie changes frustration into patience by placing the attainment of a recalcitrant outcome into the future, or much further into the future. Relieved of the pressure of immediacy, and reassured by the time available to make progress, she can trust her belief that "It will come true; I'll make it happen." To Michael, the future is a realm of unlimited possibilities, a trove of seductive "could be's" that keep him striving. Whenever he wants to feel contented, he moves from the future back to the present by paying attention to the ways in which what he has now is the best that could be.

Leslie is often kept up at night pondering all the things she *has* to do. In order to relax and go to sleep, she changes the rousing modality of necessity—what she *has* to do—to the tranquilizing modalities of wishing and possibility. In other words, she dreams about all the wonderful things she would like to do and that she could do. Michael heeds the evident lesson of the consequences of active and passive involvement by remaining determined instead of hopeful about our son Mark learning and maintaining certain personal grooming habits.

Many people are outraged by the inconveniences, incompetencies, and injustices that life deals out. A plane delay, a meal not served in time to be able to enjoy it, or the cleaners spoiling a dress can be cause for immediate and sustained anger. Leslie has learned to diffuse such anger into mild feelings of "bother" by reducing intensity. She does this by asking herself questions like, "In five years will I even be able to remember this?" If necessary, she imagines herself five or ten years in the future and, looking back from this perspective, questions why that minor nuisance ever seemed important.

Leslie uses tempo as a tonic whenever she feels harried. Whether she is rushing to meet a deadline for an article or to get dinner on the table, as soon as she realizes she is feeling harried, she slows down the tempo of her thoughts and body sensations. This slowing of tempo results in her ability to move from an agitated concern about the deadline or the dinner to once again being able to notice and to feel a sense of caring for the people around her, while continuing to accomplish the task at hand.

Michael used to feel guilty whenever he was enjoying himself if there were other things he thought he should be doing. Because he used the criterion "what should I be doing," it rarely occurred to him that time off for play could be enjoyed free of guilt. That changed when he realized he could change his criteria. Now, in the same kinds of situations, he pays attention to the fact that he is doing something he really wants to be doing, and he gets to feel deliciously naughty.

If Leslie is hurt by what someone has said or done, she changes the criterion she is using to evaluate the situation from "how I am feeling" to "what's going on with him or her." This change in filter colors her emotional response with the hues of curiosity, empathy, and understanding.

Each of the following chapters contains specific techniques that utilize the components of emotions, techniques designed to fulfill the promise of full emotional choice. But before moving on to those techniques, let us ponder a question implicitly raised by this chapter. Suppose that it was not only Leslie, Michael, and you who understood the structure of emotions. How would the world be different if *everyone* recognized that emotional experience has a structure that can be known and practically applied?

We would no longer have to stand helplessly on the sidelines, waiting for our friends and loved ones to play out their destructive or unpleasant emotions. Instead we would have the choice of doing something to change how others feel and, in so doing, how they act and how we ourselves feel. Of course, we do influence the feelings of others. We always have. But we generally wield this influence indiscriminately, like a spotlight hooked to a belt, jouncing about and haphazardly lighting this and that as we move about. In a world of emotional choice in which the community of emotional responses is understood by all, that spotlight would be hand-held, its warm illumination intentionally directed into those cold, dark emotional corners where it is most needed. In short, we would have a world in which the quest for emotional satisfaction is a cooperative pursuit, rather than a solitary labor.

# 6

# *Orienting to Your Emotions*

IN CHAPTER 3 WE INTRODUCED THE FOUR KEY ABILITIES OF emotional choice: Placement, Expression, Employment, and Prevention. Now that you are familiar with the concepts of emotional choice and the structure of emotions, it is time to learn the specific techniques for breathing life into those key abilities.

The first ability, Placement, is the process of pairing up a specific situation with the most appropriate emotions for that situation. This pairing up requires that you orient yourself to the effect of using different emotions in different situations; that you be able to select the best emotions to use for a specific situation; and that you be able to access those emotions in that situation. The methods for orienting to your emotions are covered in this chapter. Techniques for selecting and accessing emotions are presented in the following two chapters. Taken together, the techniques in this and the following two chapters compose the ability of Placement.

*Placement* ⟶ Orient Select Access
*Expression*
*Employment*
*Prevention*

To begin to select and access emotions before you orient to them would be like grabbing tools out of a toolbox to tackle a particular project without first knowing the capabilities and limitations of each tool. For example, the pipe wrench is a clever invention, but you are headed for problems if you try to use one to screw two pieces of wood together. Screwdrivers have their place, but that place is not where a hammer or saw is needed. Even tools that seem similar can have dissimilar uses. A cross-cut saw produces different results than a ripsaw. And you had better not try using either one when a pipe needs to be cut, especially if a hacksaw is at hand. Each emotion is a specialized tool that is best used to do the job for which it is best suited. In the case of emotions, each "job" or "task" is a different context, and using the wrong emotional tool in a given context can be counterproductive, or even dangerous.

By *context* we mean any situation in which you experience and express your emotions. If you are feeling frustrated while trying to study for your final exams, then the context for your frustration is *studying for final exams.* If you are feeling confident about a possible career change, then the context for your feeling of confidence is *considering a career change.* Context simply refers to the circumstances that form the environment for your emotional responses.

Context can be tremendously important in determining what kinds of emotional responses are most appropriate. In fact, many situations demand certain kinds of emotions if you are to respond in a way that is both satisfying and effective. For instance, emotions such as frustrated and challenged are appropriate when you are faced with studying for a class in which you are a little out of your depth because those emotions tend to keep you engaged in trying. Defeated and inadequate are obviously less appropriate emotions to feel when you are trying to pass a test.

The fact is, some emotions are better (in the sense of being more appropriate) in some situations than in others. True emotional choice is manifested when you are able to recognize the emotional needs of a particular situation, rather than simply responding to it and picking up the pieces later. The best way we know of to orient yourself to the emotional needs created by various contexts is to study a number of contrasting examples, such as those that follow. And the best way to get the most out of these examples is to identify situations of your own that are similar to the ones described.

For instance, you may not be studying for a difficult class (as in the previous example), but you can probably find some other current situation in which you must perform well at a task you feel ill-equipped to handle, such as making a presentation to your co-workers, coming up with a design for your new home, or establishing an intimate relationship. By personalizing each example you will not only provide yourself with important information about how to change a personally significant situation in your life, you will also teach yourself how to recognize the *situational characteristics* that create the need for certain kinds of emotions.

## *Situational Characteristics*

PATIENCE has a slow and steady tempo coupled with the maintaining of an outcome. Patience allows you to keep going, while giving you the time to evaluate and reevaluate your actions, criteria, and the goal itself as you progress. Clearly, patience is an appropriate emotion to have when your desired outcome will take time. For example, weaving is a task that can only be completed one run of yarn at a time, and so is best done with patience. Similarly, parenting children, growing a garden, teaching, and fixing or building something are contexts in which you may not be able to impose your own preferred timetable. Instead, they require patience if your experience and that of those around you is to be pleasant as you strive toward your outcome.

It is *not* appropriate to feel patient when you are presented with relatively imminent negative consequences if you do not attain your outcome. If your house is burning it's time to take action and make things happen—get help, get out, save pets, get the hose—not to feel patient. Similarly, it is generally not useful to feel patient in a situation in which you are being taken advantage of in a significant way, such as when your spouse batters you or you are repeatedly turned down for promotion. In other words, contexts in which it is or will be dangerous to let things unfold in their own time are inappropriate for feeling patient.

CALM is a wonderful emotion to feel when going to bed at night, while relaxing or meditating, or while on vacation or enjoying scenery. (Remember, we are not talking about acting calm, but about *feeling* calm.) Almost any situation in which there is nothing that you *have* to do will be enhanced by feeling calm. Of course, feeling calm becomes inappropriate when you are in a context that requires you to be immediately responsive, or in a learning situation that requires you to be alert.

Although they are similar in some respects, there is a difference between feeling calm and feeling patient. Patience requires an outcome that you are pursuing within a relatively extended time frame. Calm, on the other hand, does not require an outcome.

DETERMINATION is essential when you are trying to become physically fit, make your business successful, or get a college or graduate degree. Feeling determined can be of tremendous value whenever you are faced with making a sustained effort in order to accomplish some outcome. The narrow focus of attention that characterizes determination, and which is largely responsible for its effectiveness in helping you reach your outcomes, may also be inappropriate or harmful if it somehow threatens your personal well-being. Along with the feeling of determination comes a set of blinders that keeps you focused on your goal and relatively unaware of anything else going on around you that seems unrelated to that goal. A man who is determined to make his business a success may immerse himself in long hours, frequent business trips, and worrying about the business when at home, and fail to notice that his family relationships are being dangerously ignored or that his health is deteriorating. Feeling determined may also be a poor choice if the goal you are striving toward is, in fact, not worthwhile. Trying to make someone fall in love with you even though you know that that person does not even like you is an example of an outcome that is probably not worth pouring your time, energy, and heart into, and so is definitely not one to feel determined about.

ENCOURAGED is what you feel when you are perceiving increments of progress toward a goal. Obviously, this is an important emotion when you are striving toward a goal that will be difficult to attain, or a long time coming. Working with severely handicapped people or working for world peace are examples of contexts that usually offer a sustaining sense of progress only one small bit at a time. Weight loss is another example of an outcome that can be difficult and long term. The vigilance and restraint required when dieting are best sustained by feeling continually encouraged by such small tokens of progress as the loss of a pound this week, or the refusal of dessert at last night's dinner.

With its emphasis on increments of success, feeling encouraged is often a better choice than feeling satisfied when some part of the goal has been achieved. Satisfaction often tends to bring striving to a halt, while feeling encouraged tends to move you to the next small step. Feeling encouraged is not useful if the evidences of success are inappropriate and keep you striving toward an outcome that is not worthwhile. For instance, it is not useful to feel encouraged about getting the respect of someone who has consistently demonstrated that he has no respect for *anyone*, regardless of that person's other possible attributes or accomplishments. Nor is it useful to respond to the initial good feelings you get from alcohol or cocaine by feeling encouraged to have more.

RESIGNATION is appropriate when you must set aside what you want in order to attain an outcome that has a higher priority. For instance, you may have to resign yourself to writing a paper in order to please a teacher; or resign yourself to being alone with the kids for the weekend so that your mate can take a much needed break from the family; or resign yourself to missing a favorite television program in order to help your child with a school assignment.

When you feel resigned you do not give up what you want (as in disappointment), but merely set it aside in favor of some other outcome that is of greater importance. It is best to feel resigned only about things that are either short term or are in transition, such as writing a loathsome paper, or being alone with the kids for the weekend. It is inappropriate to feel resigned in situations that are or could be ongoing. For instance, being resigned to the fact that your spouse ridicules you daily, or that you are a paraplegic, can only lead to pent-up anger and dissatisfaction. In such situations, resignation should serve only as a temporary bridge to either determination to do something about it, as in the case of the spouse, or to acceptance, as in the case of the paraplegic.

ACCEPTANCE is something you might want to feel regarding your height of 5′2″, your parents' eternal question about when you are getting married, your daughter's penchant for punk rock, your son's disinterest in playing sports, or your best friend's habit of chewing with his mouth open. These are things that either you can't change, or that would not be worth what you would have to go through in order to try. In such situations it is often most appropriate to feel acceptance for the way things are so that you are free to devote your time and energy toward outcomes that you *can* influence. Feeling acceptance leads to disengaging you from your goal, which makes it an inappropriate emotion if it is just being used as a way of giving up on a goal that is attainable and worthwhile. For example, it is probably not appropriate to feel acceptance about having a low-paying, unsatisfying job. Unlike disappointment, acceptance is ongoing, allowing you to live comfortably with your circumstances.

FRUSTRATION can be useful when you are trying to lose weight, to get the IRS to send you a refund check or correct a computer error, to get your garden to grow in spite of poor soil, or to lick some personal problem that has been plaguing you. When you feel frustrated you are maintaining the importance of some outcome that you have in mind, and you are still trying to attain that outcome despite setbacks and difficulties. In addition, frustration is active, orienting you toward *doing* something. Frustration, then, is worth feeling when it is necessary for you to reengage or to remain engaged in striving toward some outcome.

Once you are thoroughly engaged, however, it is best to move on to some other emotion, because the unpleasantness of feeling frustrated may eventually get in the way of responding to the source of the frustration with an appropriate action. Frustration serves best as a temporary bridge to the more behaviorally effective emotions of curiosity or patience or determination. Frustration is *not* useful in situations in which you are faced with outcomes that you would be better off discarding. For instance, it is almost always useless and futile to feel frustrated about getting your adult child to live according to your wishes.

DISAPPOINTMENT is what you feel when a relationship for which you had high hopes suddenly collapses, or when you are turned down for a job that you really wanted, or when you don't get the special gift you were hoping for on your birthday. Feeling disappointed lets you know that you did not get whatever it was that you wanted. This makes it a useful emotion when it's time to let go of the pursuit of an outcome, or to let go of waiting for an outcome to be fulfilled by others. Feeling disappointed is the recognition that something is over (too late, not going to happen), and so it helps you to disengage from an outcome, thereby freeing you to move on to other pursuits. Even though a relationship is over, some people continue to feel frustrated or jealous, keeping themselves engaged in an unpleasant and useless way. Disappointment, however, brings only a passive sense of involvement, which helps to keep you from striving any further. Of course, there are times when it's important to continue striving. Feeling disappointed is inappropriate when you want to continue to pursue an outcome, such as when you have not yet gotten down to your target weight, discover that your dance lessons have not turned you into Fred Astaire, or recognize some trouble in your marriage. These are situations in which you would probably want to continue striving, at least for a while, rather than feeling disappointed and giving up on the goal.

CAUTION is the appropriate emotion to have when you are faced with a situation that is potentially dangerous, or in which it is important to minimize risk. As exhilarating as scuba diving can be, it can also be dangerous, making it imperative that a feeling of caution be included along with feelings of excitement, awe, and enjoyment. It is also useful to feel cautious if you suspect that there is reason to be jealous of your mate, since behaving rashly—by accusing, prying, or withdrawing—could unnecessarily endanger your relationship and your own well-being. Feeling cautious is of no use when you are in a situation that is familiar to you and that poses no danger, for it occupies much of your consciousness with calculations about how to avoid or respond to possible dangers. Feeling cautious can dull your enjoyment of such things as talking with friends, dancing, or taking an afternoon stroll.

SUSPICION is what you feel when an acquaintance who you *know* hates you is suddenly and inexplicably friendly. In such a situation you recognize a significant mismatch between the other person's past behavior and her present behavior toward you. Similarly, a contractor who promises to do your job twice as fast as anyone else, but who has a reputation for dragging out jobs, might elicit suspicion. Or you might feel suspicious when a fellow employee, who has repeatedly divulged your private and potentially embarrassing conversations to your superiors, professes her friendly feelings for you. Feeling suspicious is useful when you are with people who can harm you, know they can harm you, and yet are treating you as though nothing is amiss. The difference between feeling suspicious and feeling skeptical is one of intensity. It is the perception of great harm that promotes skepticism to the more protective suspicion.

Suspicion is a very inappropriate emotion, however, if there is no evidence of a mismatch between the other person's past and present behavior. The impact of feeling suspicious is to motivate you to both remain at arm's length and to search for confirming evidence of dishonesty. Feeling suspicious when there is no danger of harm and no evidence of a mismatch will only lead you to behaviors guaranteed to create confusion, resentment, and anger in others.

## *Learning to Orient*

The ability to think about your emotions in terms of their usefulness in relation to certain situations is vital to having emotional choice. It's a matter of finding "the right tool for the right job," as the old adage has it. You have just read a number of examples of various emotions and the situations for which they are generally appropriate and inappropriate. Now you will have the opportunity to make the idea of orientation relevant to your personal experiences and unique situations, as well as to become even more familiar and at ease with the process of finding the best emotional tool for a given situation. For your convenience, we have included the following format for orienting to your emotions (as well as all other formats presented in subsequent chapters), with each step separately numbered, in the "Formats at a Glance" section at the end of the book.

To personalize your emotional orientation, you begin by identifying a situation or context that frequently elicits an emotional reaction in you—for instance, studying for exams, fighting rush-hour traffic, cooking dinner, playing with the children, getting out reports, exercising, or reading technical manuals. You then need to learn to discover the different consequences of different emotions by applying various emotions to that situation, and then considering what your response might be. We suggest you do this by considering the emotions and the situation in the following way.

First, identify a familiar situation. Imagine yourself in that situation, clearly and in detail. What do you see? What do you hear? When you have firmly established the scene, select an emotion. Imagine feeling that emotion in that familiar situation to discover what your response would be. When you have thoroughly explored your reaction, select another emotion and imagine feeling it in the same context. How does your reaction to the situation change in response to the new emotion?

Holding the situation constant, you can run through as many emotions as you wish, observing the variations in your response.

Once you have established the situation, you can use the following question for your explorations.

> *If I feel* ___(emotion)___ *in this situation, what will be the consequences?*

So for instance:

> If you felt "curious" as a student it would *keep you engaged* in learning.
>
> If you felt "inadequate" as a student it would lead you to *less participation*, *more worry*, *doubt*, and *confusion*.
>
> If you felt "stubborn" as a student it would get you into *arguments* about material or course requirements.
>
> If you felt "apathy" as a student you would *miss what of value was going on* since you would be so disengaged.

In each case, you keep the context the same, changing only the emotion you are feeling. Then imagine how feeling that way would affect your experience and behavior. Try to come up with emotions for each context that will produce behaviors that are *useful*, as well as emotions that will lead to *nonuseful* or *detrimental* behaviors. Here are several more examples to stimulate your thinking.

*The Situation: Meeting New People*

If you felt "friendly" you would *make contact* and *be engaged.*

If you felt "awe" you *wouldn't interact naturally or be yourself.*

If you felt "apprehensive" you would *hold back* and *be hesitant in expressing yourself.*

If you felt "suspicious" you would generate defensive or even offensive behaviors, such as *arrogance* and *snide comments.*

*The Situation: Taking a Test*

If you felt "ambitious" you would *apply yourself* and perhaps *do more than required.*

If you felt "competent" you would take the test in a *relaxed* manner, *taking your time*, and have *better access to your knowledge.*

If you felt "terror" you *couldn't access your knowledge* and would *do horribly.*

If you felt "restless" you would make *careless mistakes.*

If you felt "apathetic" you *wouldn't apply yourself.*

*The Situation: Job Interview*

If you felt "encouraged" you would *relax*, *feel confident*, *speak up*, and *act in a way that is congruent with your abilities.*

If you felt "alert" you would *tune in* to what the interviewer is after and make more *internal assessments* about what to say and do.

If you felt "anxious" you would *sweat* and *fail to convey your best attributes* to the interviewer.

## *The Situation: Catching an Airplane*

If you felt "exuberant" you would *enjoy the trip* to the airport and *look forward to meeting people* on the plane.

If you felt "anxious" you would be *on time* but *would fret and miss out on interesting things going on with the people around you.*

If you felt "dread" you would be *tempted to miss the flight* and *be sure to have money for drinks and the in-flight movie and plenty of magazines to get lost in.*

Of course, how *you* would respond and behave when feeling the emotions suggested in these examples may be different than the possibilities described. Just how you respond when feeling a certain way in a particular situation is determined by your unique personal history, personality, and resources.

If you haven't already done it, go ahead and select a context that is familiar to you and imagine how your responses would change as you vary the emotions you are feeling in that context. Remember to find an example of an emotion that would lead you to a useful response, and one that would lead to a nonuseful or detrimental response. Repeat this exploration for at least five different contexts that are of significance to you. Being criticized or complimented are good ones to try.

From our examples and your own explorations, it should be apparent that your emotions in a particular situation have a great deal to do with your experience and behavior in that situation, and furthermore that some emotions are more appropriate and useful than others for a given situation. The emotions that you want and need to have are those that maximize both the quality of your experience and your effectiveness in securing your outcomes. We next turn to presenting the means by which you can identify just which emotions are the "maximizing" ones for you.

# 7

# *Selecting Your Emotions*

WHEN YOU ARE PLANNING A TRIP TO A FOREIGN COUNTRY you can get books that tell you what to pack for your adventure, but there are none that tell you what emotions to bring along. What feeling should you bring to the exploration of a new land? Patience? Acceptance? Curiosity? Suspicion? Fascination? Challenge? Adventure? Caution? We know one voyager, Steve, whose initial choice was to work himself up into a state of excitement over being in a foreign country. Steve soon discovered, however, that his excitement kept his tempo so fast that he was unable to make contact and interact with the people in that culture, which he very much wanted to do. So Steve shifted to the relatively slower tempo of curiosity, and soon found himself invited to spend the evening in people's homes.

Why are there no travel guides that tell you what emotions to pack for your travels, whether your journey is to new countries, new personal relationships, or new professional successes? The answer is that most of us assume that we have no choice about how we respond emotionally in various situations. For most people, an emotion is something that happens *to* them as a response to whatever is going on at the time. Most people never think to choose their emotions. The fact is, however, that you *can* choose your emotions; given the choice, people usually choose well for themselves.

This chapter is about the selection of emotions. Once you are able to make an informed choice about what emotions will be most appropriate for you in a particular situation, you will be able to act on that choice, adjusting your feelings accordingly.

Everyone can think of many personal examples of feeling an emotion that was inappropriate to the situation and to the desired outcome. Perhaps you were involved in the delivery of a baby and felt exhilarated when, in terms of assisting the birth, it would have been more appropriate to feel responsible. Or perhaps you moved to an unstructured work situation in which you wanted to feel free and behave responsibly, but instead felt contented and got nothing done.

Given that it is possible to choose and to choose well (in a way that facilitates pleasure and effectiveness), the question is, How do you go about choosing an appropriate emotion? There are three times when this question is relevant: *before* you are about to step into a new role or situation; when you discover that your feelings and behaviors are other than what you would like them to be *during* an experience; and when you realize *after* an experience that you did not respond the way you would have liked. We will look at these instances one at a time, providing for each one a *selection format* you can use to give yourself emotional choice.

## *After*

Remember the last time you were stuck in traffic, impotently raging at three miles of cars that were just as stuck as you were? Or the vacation when you went ahead and unloaded the sacks of concrete even though you were already tired, and hurt your back? Or that Christmas when you insisted that your family open their presents on your cue so that you could record their pleasure with your new VCR, and thereby spoiled the spontaneity of Christmas morning? And who could forget, although you would like to, the job interview in which you were so humble and self-effacing that you humbled yourself right out of the job? Or the night you hollered at your daughter to finish her homework, upsetting her so much that she was unable to finish her homework? Or, well, the time you treated your mate to a weekend of vicious and suspicious sarcasm because he or she had met an old flame for lunch?

Those moments that you look back on and realize "I blew it" are all too common. Sometimes you are not aware during an interaction that you aren't having the experience that you would really rather have. It's only later, when you are no longer occupied with coping with the situation itself, that you are free to look back and realize that what you felt and how you acted at the time somehow blighted the experience you had hoped for.

Of course, such experiences are water under the proverbial bridge once they have occurred. But it is unwise to neglect the probability of more "water" coming. Your future will probably hold more traffic jams, more sacks of concrete, more job interviews, and more children reluctant to do their homework. The best use of a past unpleasant experience is as a learning opportunity. You need to make sure that the next time you are in a similar situation you respond in a way that is more in accord with your desires.

Charlie, a client of ours, recently had occasion to learn about using his unpleasant experience as an opportunity to change. He explained to us that at a staff meeting at the school where he teaches the principal had attacked Charlie's restructuring of his classes as "irresponsible" and "unprofessional." Charlie flushed and sputtered as he tried to justify his program, but in the end he felt humiliated and acted in a way that was guiltily defensive. He told us that this was not the first time he had felt and acted that way in this kind of situation, but that he sure would like it to be the last. When asked how he would rather have behaved when attacked by his principal, Charlie answered that he would have preferred to respond "articulately and intelligently, to hold my own—and to discourage him from ever making such an attack again." We then asked Charlie what he would have preferred to feel, and he answered, "I think if I had felt secure in my own competence, I could have handled it much better."

We had Charlie replay the dressing down in his imagination, but this time responding from a position of feeling secure and competent. He observed that those feelings would have made a big difference in his handling of the situation. Specifically, he would not have been so rattled by the accusations, and he would have responded by calmly asking the principal questions that both addressed the accusations and questioned the appropriateness of the *principal's* behavior—though in a respectful way.

Satisfied about the past, we next had Charlie imagine responding out of feelings of security and competence in a similar incident in the future, and he was satisfied that these were indeed appropriate emotions for him to have in such a situation. Finally, we made sure that Charlie could get to the feelings of security and competence when he needed them.

It is usually not enough to simply *wish* that you had done something other than what you did. Charlie had often wished that he stood up for himself better, but that did little to fortify him when his principal attacked him. Because our emotions are so compelling in determining how we behave, it is much easier and more effective to change our behaviors by changing the emotions that generate those behaviors. With that in mind, the following format (that is, a sequence of steps) is intended to provide you with a way of selecting, for the future, emotions that are more satisfying and effective than those you have used in given situations in the past.

1. Identify an experience you had with which you are now dissatisfied because of your feelings and/or your behavior at the time; then evaluate what happened in terms of "What was going on?" and "What did I want?" (The answers to these questions could include emotions, behaviors, or outcomes.)
2. Determine how you would have liked to behave.
3. Now make your best guess at what emotion you would need to feel in order to generate that behavior.

4. Once you find an emotion that you think would have helped you behave as you would have liked, imagine that same kind of situation occurring in the future and, holding constant the emotion you have selected, imagine how it will affect your experience and behavior. Be sure to include in your consideration the responses of others, the preservation of your own well-being, and your effectiveness in achieving desired outcomes. If the emotion you have selected seems inappropriate or insufficient, then cycle back to step 3 and either choose a different emotion or add another to the one you have already selected.

5. If the emotion you have selected fulfills your desired outcome for that particular situation, be sure you have access to it so that you can feel the way you want to feel the next time you find yourself in that situation. (Accessing emotions is the subject of the next chapter.)

This sequence orients you toward thinking about your experience and behavior as *natural consequences* of certain emotions. It also orients you toward attaining your outcomes as a natural consequence of your experience and behavior. Let's use Charlie's experience with his principal as an example of what takes place at each step in this format.

Charlie had been berated by a superior in front of co-workers during a meeting. Looking back, he realized that he had felt humiliated and acted defensively.

He would prefer to have responded articulately and intelligently, to have held his own, and to have discouraged the principal from ever making such an attack again. When he thought about what he would rather have felt at the time, Charlie decided on secure and competent. He thought that these feelings would have made it possible for him to respond the way he would have liked to.

Charlie then replayed the situation in his imagination, but this time from the perspective of feeling secure and competent. With such emotions, the difference he saw in his own behavior was in accord with how he would prefer to have responded.

Charlie then imagined being in the same kind of situation in the near future, but again feeling secure and competent. He discovered that these emotions continued to produce the behaviors that were in alignment with what he wanted for himself.

Using the techniques presented in the next chapter, he then went about making sure that he had access to those emotions when he would need them.

This "After" format gets you to specify just what your desired outcome was, and will be the next time, for a particular context. It then leads you to discover which emotions will produce the experiences and behaviors you want in that situation.

As another example, imagine that you are looking back on a conversation you had earlier in the day with a new acquaintance. You realize that you felt very awkward and unsure of yourself at the time. In considering what was going on, you can see now that your new friend was responding to you far more sincerely and effusively than you had expected she would.

You decide that you would rather have responded graciously, expressing appreciation of her in return. You would prefer to have felt worthy and giving. You imagine how you would have responded to that person if at the time you had felt worthy and giving, and you realize that you would have accepted her praise graciously and would have felt comfortable with expressing your appreciation of her.

As you imagine being in that same kind of situation again in the future, responding out of the emotions of worthy and giving, you determine that those emotions are, indeed, appropriate for you and the outcomes you desire in that context. You then make sure that you have access to those emotions so that you can respond the way you have just determined will be best.

It's possible that you will go through this format without hitting upon an emotion or combination of emotions that fulfills your desired experiences and outcomes. If that happens, you need to gather more information regarding appropriate ways to respond in the situation you are concerned about. Furthermore, each time you select an inappropriate emotion you will learn something new and worthwhile with respect to the appropriate placement of your emotions.

For instance, Geri had tried to feel excited and amused when she visited her spiteful, envious sister. When Geri discovered that her feelings of excitement and amusement around her sister inevitably decayed into anger and frustration, she realized that she would have to try a different way of responding. From this experience she discovered that it was much more appropriate for her to feel patient and accepting when around her sister. Even a mistaken selection is an opportunity to learn something about that emotion in particular and about the placement of emotions in general. When used as a learning opportunity, your mistaken selection will become a source of personal pride, satisfaction, and reassurance.

## *During*

Do you ever find yourself feeling and behaving in ways that are inappropriate and unsatisfactory? For instance, you are sitting at the school board meeting, wanting to get up and make a point, but you don't because you're paralyzed by fear and uncertainty; or your children are running around the supermarket and you find yourself impotently screaming at them; or your spouse has ignored your good advice and thrown his back out gardening, and you want to feel sympathetic or caring but instead feel righteous and say some cruel things; or you want to ask for help that you really need, but your feelings of humiliation and incompetence keep you from making your needs known. These are times when you are *in* a situation and discover that how you are feeling and what you are doing is other than what you would like.

Upon finding ourselves in such circumstances, many of us believe—or at least act as though—we have no choice but to wait for the mood to pass, essentially relying upon changes in the environment to create changes in our feelings and behaviors. Frozen at the meeting, we hope that someone else will voice our opinions so that we will feel emboldened. In the supermarket we try to get the kids under control so that we can get ourselves under control. Or we try to get our spouse to follow our advice so that we will not have to feel righteous and act cruelly. Or we hope that the person whose help we are seeking will recognize our unspoken need and encourage us to speak up. Of course, the problem with depending on the environment changing is that it may not oblige.

Leslie was out to dinner in a posh restaurant, but she was not enjoying herself. She felt intimidated by the hovering wine steward and the pretentious surroundings. Excusing herself, she left her companions to get a breath of fresh air. Once outside, Leslie felt more at ease. Thinking about the scene inside the restaurant, she realized that there was really nothing to feel intimidated about. When she asked herself what she wanted for herself when she returned to the dining room, her answer was, "to enjoy the experience and the people I'm with." Leslie then considered what she would need to feel in order to enjoy the evening, and decided that she needed to feel "a sense of belonging" and "pleasant anticipation." Leslie is at ease with her surroundings when she feels that she belongs, and she tends to be animated and talkative when she feels pleasant anticipation.

Wanting to be sure of her conclusion before stepping back into the intimidating world of wine stewards and white gloves, she imagined feeling a sense of belonging and of pleasant anticipation when she returned. She knew those feelings would make a big difference in her ability to enjoy the evening. Satisfied, Leslie returned to her table, this time doing what she needed to do in order to feel that sense of belonging and of pleasant anticipation.

In reality, *you are not shackled to your current emotions*. Of course, when you realize that what you are doing and feeling is not what you want, you could just ride out the unpleasantness, then turn to the After format once you finally escape the situation. Leslie could have endured her evening of intimidation and then, back home, figured out how to ensure that she doesn't have to go through that same unpleasantness in the future. But at the time she realized she was feeling intimidated she was in the restaurant and she wanted to be having a nice time. Seeing no reason to throw away the evening, Leslie did what she needed to do in order to change how she was responding. *When you recognize that your ongoing experience is not what you would like it to be, you have the choice of changing it*. The following format provides you with a way of identifying what change of emotion you need to fulfill your experiential and behavioral goals in any situation.

1. When you become aware that your current experience is somehow unsatisfactory, specify just how you are feeling and behaving in this situation.

2. Take a deep breath, then "step away from yourself." (In your imagination, see yourself in the situation, thus

becoming a detached spectator for the moment.) From this detached perspective, ask yourself, "What do I want? What is my desired outcome?"

3. Select one or more feelings that would be more useful in getting what you want in the current situation.
4. Identify what behaviors are the *natural consequences* of the emotion that you want to feel in this situation. That is, what are the behaviors that you naturally engage in when feeling that emotion? Are these behaviors ones that will work to your benefit in getting what you want? If the answer is no, then cycle back to step 3 and choose a different emotion you might want to have in this situation.
5. Imagine feeling the emotion that you have selected, and consider how events are likely to proceed with you feeling that way. Be sure to include in your consideration the responses of others, the preservation of your own well-being, and effectiveness in achieving your desired outcomes. If the emotion you have selected is not enough to satisfy your needs, cycle back to step 3 and add any other emotions that you think will be appropriate.
6. Shift to a means of accessing the emotion(s) you want to have in the ongoing situation. (Remember, accessing emotions is the subject of the next chapter.)

This format subjectively removes you from the unsatisfactory situation, providing you with a breather and an opportunity to consider, from a detached perspective, what is going on and what might be a better choice for you. As an example of the use of the format, here are the steps that Leslie took to change her state.

Leslie is out to dinner in a posh restaurant when she realizes that she feels intimidated by the pretentious surroundings. She "steps out" of the situation (literally, in this case), and decides that she wants "to enjoy the experience and the people I'm with."

As she thinks about the dinner party, she decides that the emotions she wants to be feeling are belonging and pleasant anticipation. Leslie knows that when she feels that she belongs she is at ease with those around her, and she is outgoing and responsive; and that when she feels pleasant anticipation she tends to be animated and talkative.

She imagines going through the evening feeling belonging and pleasant anticipation, and decides that these emotions will indeed help her fulfill her desire to have an enjoyable dining and social experience. Leslie then accesses those feelings in herself, and so changes the course of her evening.

For Leslie, making a dramatic change in her evening's experience was a direct result of separating herself from what was going on for the few moments it took to select what emotions would naturally lead her to the kind of experience she preferred. The time it took to change her whole evening could be measured in seconds. Doesn't it seem better to take a few seconds out so that you can get what you want for the rest of the evening, than to needlessly endure an unpleasant experience?

Here is another example of the During format. Let's say that you are trudging your way through household chores, feeling dreary and bored. You "step out" from your labors and decide that what you want is to get them done well, and as quickly and pleasantly as possible.

It seems to you that it would be appropriate to feel purposeful and pleased that you are getting the chores done; or, perhaps, to feel pleasant anticipation of being finished. When you feel purposeful you relentlessly pursue fulfilling your responsibilities, but without being frenetic or compulsive. Feeling pleased always cheers you and makes you eager to keep doing whatever has been the source of pleasing you. All of these behavioral consequences are in accord with what you want for yourself while cleaning house.

As a check, you imagine cleaning house with the emotional orientation of purposeful and pleased, and find that those emotions will indeed provide the basis for the kind of experience you want to have while doing your housework. You access those feelings in yourself, and so go about finishing your housework in a more pleasant frame of mind and in a more effective way.

If you cycle through the During format three times without hitting upon an emotion that fulfills your needs, then excuse yourself from the situation and consider in private whether to continue being in that situation, to gather more information, or to leave. For instance, if you are at a wedding reception and feeling very uncomfortable, you could retire to the bathroom or go outside for a stroll in order to give yourself a few moments of peace to sort out your needs.

These examples have given you a handle on the format, but the more you take yourself through it with examples of your own, the more understandable and accessible it will become. Although it takes many words to describe, actually using the format is very simple and straightforward and requires surprisingly little time.

## *Before*

There have been, and will continue to be, roles and situations that are new to you, but to which you must nevertheless respond. With the birth of a child you might suddenly find yourself in the new role of mother, grandmother, godmother, father, or uncle. With a change in job you might be faced with the novel role of manager, employee, or consultant. Similarly, dating, coming into or out of money, returning to or leaving school, living in a foreign culture or in a different cultural subgroup, and going to the opera for the first time are all potentially new experiences, often requiring new emotional orientations and behaviors.

When a situation or a role is new to you, you may not have a very good idea of just how you should approach it in terms of your emotions. For instance, should you approach your first date with a new person with feelings of dread? Caution? Curiosity? Confidence? Satisfaction? When you don't know how best to approach a new situation, you may react with those emotions that you normally feel in similar situations, rather than selecting how you would prefer to respond, and then making that a reality. You may face that first date with the familiar but unpleasant emotion of fear and perhaps end up creating an evening to forget. How much better to have gone on that date feeling, say, curious.

When Martin came to us he was feeling quite apprehensive. He was about to begin scuba diving lessons and, although he very much wanted to do it, the idea of being underwater for such long periods of time, completely dependent upon a life support system, scared him. Not wanting to go into the sport with those feelings, he came to us for help. We asked him what he wanted to accomplish in his scuba lessons, and he answered, "Have a good time and remain safe—definitely remain safe—and just see what it's like." Martin had an easy time answering "safe" and "secure" when we next asked him how he wanted to feel while taking his diving lessons. Then:

**Authors:** So Martin, how do you behave when you are feeling safe and secure?
**Martin:** I kind of space out. I "go with the flow," as they say.
**Authors:** Is that compatible with what you want your experience to be when you go diving?
**Martin:** No.
**Authors:** Why not?
**Martin:** Are you kidding? If I felt safe and secure I might do something foolish. I guess if I really want to feel safe and secure I might as well stay on the beach and sunbathe.
**Authors:** So how *do* you want to feel?
**Martin:** Well, not scared—it's a pretty big ocean out there. More like alert, and maybe intrigued or fascinated.
**Authors:** And the consequences for you of feeling alert and intrigued or fascinated?
**Martin:** Paying attention to what's going on. That's when I start seeing the adventure, but still kind of keep track of what is going on.

Combining the emotions of alert and intrigued or fascinated seemed to lead Martin to the kind of experiences he wanted to have while diving. To check this out, we had Martin imagine going through his dive training and first dives while feeling alert and intrigued. When he did this he discovered that those emotions would, indeed, fulfill his desire for a good, safe, and explorative time while learning to dive. We then turned to helping him have access to the feelings of alertness and fascination.

When you can determine how best to orient your feelings *before* you step into a new situation, as Martin was able to do with scuba diving, you create a high degree of flexibility and choice for yourself. When you establish an experiential outcome in terms of emotions, your own experience provides the feedback to know if you are on track. The following format will help you to select your most appropriate and satisfying emotions in a future situation.

1. Describe the situation, specifically including what about it is familiar and what about it is new and unfamiliar to you.
2. Consider what you want to accomplish in this situation, even if it is only to enjoy yourself, or to be helpful, or to protect yourself.
3. Decide what you want to feel in this situation.
4. Identify what behaviors are natural consequences of the emotion that you would like to feel in this situation. That is, what are the behaviors that you naturally engage in when feeling that emotion?

   Are these behaviors ones you want in the upcoming situation? Are they compatible with the outcomes that you have set for the situation? If the answer is no, then cycle back to step 3 and choose a different emotion you might want to have in this situation.
5. Imagine being in the upcoming situation, feeling the emotion that you have selected, and evaluate how events are likely to proceed. Be sure to include in your evaluation the responses of others, the preservation of your own well-being, and your effectiveness in achieving desired outcomes. If the emotion you have selected is not enough to satisfy your needs, cycle back to step 3 and add any other emotions that you think will be appropriate.
6. Shift to a means of accessing the emotion(s) you want to have in the upcoming situation. (You will learn methods for accessing emotions in the next chapter.)

This sequence provides you with a way of assessing ahead of time how best to orient your emotions so that your experience will be what you want it to be. It will also help ensure that you attain the goals you have set for yourself in a particular situation. This is the same sequence that we took Martin through to help him have the kind of diving experience he wanted to have.

Martin is preparing to take diving lessons. He has learned new sports before, but what is new about this experience is being underwater for long periods of time and being dependent on a life support system. What he wants to accomplish includes having a good time, remaining safe, and seeing what it's like.

While learning to dive he wants to feel safe and secure. Asked what his behavior is when he feels safe and secure, Martin replies that he "spaces out" and "just goes with the flow." (These are, for him, the natural behavioral consequences of feeling safe and secure.) He then considers the compatibility of these behaviors with respect to his goal of remaining safe ("I might do something foolish"), and realizes that safe and secure are not the emotions he needs to be feeling.

Reconsidering his choice of emotions, Martin decides that perhaps he needs to feel alert and intrigued or fascinated. When feeling these emotions, Martin both pays attention and experiences the adventure. This is in accord with his desired outcomes for the diving lessons. To check this out, Martin imagines going through his dive training and first dives while feeling alert and intrigued. He discovers that the behavioral orientation that those emotions provide will help him fulfill his desire for a safe and enjoyable diving experience. Martin then learns how to access the feelings of alertness and fascination in the context of diving.

Here is another example of the format in use. Mary, one of our trainees, is going to a seminar and, although she has been to many seminars before, the topic of this one is unfamiliar to her. What will be new to her about this seminar is the specific concept being presented and the other people attending.

Mary wants to determine whether or not the concept is useful and, if so, learn how to use it, and she wants to connect with other participants as possible professional resources and as personal friends. She decides that at the workshop she wants to feel comfortable. When she considers the natural consequences of the emotion she has chosen, Mary realizes that feeling comfortable will make her laid back. When she asks herself if that behavior will be useful at the workshop, the answer is, "No, that won't get me what I really want." So she cycles back and selects curious and friendly as possibly better choices for how to orient her feelings.

Mary then considers the natural consequences of these emotions and realizes that when she feels curious she is engaged in learning and speculation about how to use things, and that when she is feeling friendly she tends to initiate contact with, and be responsive to, others. The natural consequences of feeling curious and friendly, then, are likely to orient Mary in such a way as to satisfy her desire to assess and learn, as well as to get to know the other people attending the seminar.

As a final check, Mary imagines being at the seminar, participating in what is going on there while maintaining the emotions of curiosity and friendliness. When she does this she can see herself "doing great." That is, she is engaged in learning and in pursuing contact with others, and others are responding well to her.

Finally, Mary adopts a method for guaranteeing that she will feel the way she wants to when she actually finds herself at the seminar.

By taking herself through this sequence, Mary has provided herself with the opportunity to select her emotional orientation before stepping into the seminar situation, rather than showing up and merely reacting, perhaps inappropriately, to what she finds there. Step 4 in the format gets you to attend both to the kinds of behaviors that will make it possible for you to fulfill the experiences you want to have and to the kinds of emotions that, for you, naturally give you access to those behaviors. The few moments that Mary spent asking and answering the format questions created for her, as it can for you, the possibility of choice.

If you have cycled through the format three times without feeling satisfied with the emotion(s) you have selected, then you need to gather more information from someone who has been in the situation that you will be stepping into. For instance, if you are feeling "scared" or "intimidated" about being called as a trial witness for the first time, try to speak with someone who not only has been a trial witness, but also managed to be comfortable, to enjoy it, and to find it rewarding. Find out from this person what you can expect and what his or her emotions were when he or she did well. You can use that information as a guide. And you may find that the emotions he or she experienced will serve you just as well.*

## *What You Have Now*

Most people either tolerate their unwanted emotions or do their best to avoid situations that summon them up. They don't have a choice about their emotions because it has never occurred to

* For more information about gathering information from others on which to model your own responses, see *The EMPRINT Method: A Guide to Reproducing Competence*, by Cameron-Bandler, Gordon, and Lebeau.

them to choose. But it *is* possible. You now have a means of selecting useful and desirable emotions for yourself. The formats make this possible. You now have a format you can use *before* you enter into a situation that is unfamiliar, one you can use *during* a situation in which you are not feeling and acting the way you would like to, and one you can use *after* a less than satisfying experience to change how you respond in that situation in the future. You can select your emotions and thereby control your own experience to an extent that is far beyond the ability of most people.

With that experiential control comes true choice. Everyone knows what it is like to feel an emotion that is inappropriate, shoving you out of alignment with your current wants and needs. Being able to select your emotions, however, means that you can choose whatever feeling is most in alignment with what you are doing. *All* of you will "be there." With all of you in sync with the moment, you can better focus on fulfilling your desired outcomes, instead of coping with unpleasant and inappropriate emotions. This greater congruence means the ability to be more of who you are, feeling the way you want to feel as you move through the world. And those around you will receive a double benefit. They not only get to know you better by being able to see you feeling and behaving as you *are*, but they get to respond to a congruent you, rather than struggling to understand and appropriately interact with someone who is incongruent. And finally, the freedom that comes with being able to choose makes it possible for you to generate possible outcomes for yourself that you might not otherwise have considered, simply because those outcomes involved emotional choices that seemed to be beyond you.

What if everyone had the ability to select their emotions? Of course, everyone would be operating much more at their best and in a more congruent way. The result would be more accurate understanding and communication, making it more possible for people to work cooperatively. In addition, all of us would get better and better at judging what is worth feeling because we would have constant opportunities to observe and participate in the testing and contrasting of emotions. In short, all of us would be involved in learning about the range of human emotion and experience, with all of us as students, and all of us as teachers.

# 8

# *Accessing Your Emotions*

WE WERE DRIVING DOWN A FREEWAY WHEN MICHAEL WAS suddenly cut off in traffic by an eighteen-wheeler changing lanes without signalling. Michael turned crimson as he glared at the offender, cursing through gritted teeth. A moment later, he took a deep breath, relaxed back in his seat, and grinned sardonically. When asked what he had just done inside to change his emotional state, Michael explained, "Whenever I get hot like that I repeat inside my head two rules for preventing heart disease that I read in a book: 'Don't sweat the small stuff,' and 'Everything is small stuff.' Then I just take a deep breath and things are much better."

Amazingly, Michael had decided to change how he was feeling and then he just did it. Once you have selected what, for you, will be a satisfying and appropriate emotion, you must have a way of getting to or *accessing* that emotion when you need and want it. Once they know what to go for, people are often able to access the emotions they need. Knowing what you want as your outcome in a situation, plus knowing what kind of emotions would naturally lead you to respond in a way that is in accord with that outcome, may be all the reorientation and impetus you need to put your choice into effect.

Sometimes, however, you know how you want to feel but are unable to initiate those feelings in yourself. We are aware of dozens of methods of accessing emotions in ourselves and in others, but all of them are variations of four basic approaches. Rather than discussing dozens of methods, let's go directly to those four underlying approaches.

## *Tapping Your Emotions*

The first approach relies on your familiarity with your own emotional experience and the ways you have of affecting that experience. Simply stated, you access the feelings you need by generating in yourself the kinds of experiences or behaviors that you know usually lead you to have the emotions you are after. It is said that the surrealist painter Rene Magritte, to prepare himself emotionally for his day's work at home, would dress impeccably, take up his briefcase and kiss his wife goodbye, then walk around the block and reenter his house, ready to work.

It may be that before picking up this book you had not thought in terms of having emotional choice and control. The foundations of emotional choice, however, can be found in all of us. Looking back over the last week you can undoubtedly find examples of situations in which you felt one way, then changed your thinking or what you were doing in such a way that how you were feeling changed as well. Often these unintentional instances of emotional choice go by without your noticing that you *did* something, even if inadvertently, that changed how you felt.

Because we tend to take for granted the daily emotional changes we make in ourselves, it may be easier for you initially to recognize the ability that other people have to change their emotional state, such as Michael on the freeway and Magritte at work. Reviewing again the past week, perhaps you can find examples of people who were obviously in the throes of some unpleasant emotion and then, in a few moments time, seemed to make some internal adjustments in themselves, to reemerge feeling and acting differently. For instance, we know a woman who has very specific—and somewhat expensive—ideas about the kind of home she eventually wants to own. Often she begins to feel discouraged, or even hopeless. As soon as she recognizes that happening, however, she starts making vivid pictures in her head of "how it is going to be someday," and she shifts her emotional state to feeling ambitious once again.

Another woman whose five young children occasionally get her feeling rattled, exasperated, and angry, takes a moment to remember how innocent and precious they look when sleeping. These memories touch off a warm feeling in her chest, which she then feels spreading throughout her body. The result for her is a feeling of patience and a renewed sense of humor. When it comes to feeling discouraged, or rattled, these people have emotional choice. That is, they are aware of effective ways of changing their feelings, and they use them.

The key to tapping your emotions is to discover how *you* naturally go about changing your feelings, and how others change their emotions in ways that might work as well for you. To begin with, we suggest that you find recent examples of times when you changed your emotional state, either intentionally or unintentionally, then discover just what you did in your behavior or internal experience to bring about that change.

To give you an idea of the wide range of ways there are to adjust your experience and behavior in order to affect your feelings, consider these possible ways of going for feeling confident.

CONFIDENT

- □ Adjust your body posture to one that is confident.
- □ Remember a time when you felt and acted confident.
- □ Talk to yourself, telling yourself that you're great, reminding yourself of things that you appreciate about you.
- □ See yourself doing something amazing, such as climbing a mountain or flying a plane.

- □ Identify something within the situation that you are already confident about.
- □ Feel your own backbone, and feel as though it were a steel rod.
- □ Identify a clear outcome for yourself in the situation.
- □ Play a particularly affecting piece of music in your head, one that makes you feel confident.
- □ Think of people who make you feel confident and imagine them small and sitting on your shoulder, talking into your ear.

What ways do *you* have of making yourself feel confident? As you can see from the list above, there are certainly many ways to do it. Now suppose that you want to feel composed when faced with a situation in which it would be better to respond thoughtfully rather than react rashly; or curious when you are bored and want to be involved; or amused when you are taking things too seriously.

COMPOSED

- □ Picture a still, quiet body of water.
- □ Imagine yourself in a Japanese garden.
- □ Take a deep breath, close your eyes, and readjust your posture.
- □ Listen to slow, calming, harmonious music inside your head.
- □ Clasp your hands together and think about unity.
- □ Count slowly to ten.

CURIOUS

- □ Ask yourself questions that you really care about getting the answers to, especially questions having to do with what is going on around you at the time.
- □ Ask others such questions as, "How do you do that?" and "How does that work?"

- □ Change your body posture so that it is more forward, more engaged.
- □ Think of getting answers to questions without actually asking those questions out loud.
- □ Search for answers and patterns in the things going on around you.

AMUSED

- □ Imagine having super powers but not using them on mere mortals.
- □ Imagine everyone running around in diapers.
- □ Think of outrageous things to say, without any intention of actually saying them.
- □ Generate puns, and keep them to yourself or say them aloud.
- □ Look for ambiguities in the things people say.
- □ Imagine this same situation from a different time frame—perhaps ten years in the future or ten years in the past.
- □ Imagine what your favorite comedian would do in the situation.

The lists above are intended only as examples. Although some of our suggestions might work very well for you, remember that you probably already have in place your own ways of generating these emotions in yourself—ways that, for you, *naturally* take you to the emotion.

As you read through the examples above you may have noticed that they fall into various categories. You can "tap" an emotion using:

| | |
|---|---|
| *A Memory* | "Confident." Remember a time when you felt and acted confident. |
| *A Fantasy* | "Amused." Imagine having super powers but not using them on mere mortals. |

| | |
|---|---|
| *Adjusting Your Body* | "Curious." Change your body posture so that it is more forward, more engaged. |
| *Redirecting Attention* | "Confident." Identify a clear outcome for yourself in the situation. |
| *Changing Time Frame* | "Amused." Imagine this same situation from ten years in the future or ten years in the past. |
| *Changing Intensity* | "Composed." Listen to slow, calming, harmonious music inside your head. |
| *Changing Tempo* | "Composed." Count slowly to ten. |
| *Changing Involvement* | "Curious." Search for answers and patterns in the things going on around you. |
| *Changing Criteria* | "Motivated." Keep in mind the importance of caring for your family. |
| *Changing Chunk Size* | "Capable." Divide an overwhelming task into smaller, more manageable tasks. |
| *Looking For What Is Missing or What Is There* | "Curious." Ask yourself questions that you really care about getting the answers to. |

These are all ways of affecting your own experience; they can provide you with the means through which you can access the emotions you need and want.

*An important note: Do NOT use drugs or food as your way of getting to the emotional states you want. Using substances as a means of changing your feelings leads to dependencies and unfortunate, even disastrous, secondary consequences, such as inability to function, mood swings, high blood pressure, cancer, or obesity.*

In addition to your own experiences, the experiences of other people will teach you a great deal about how emotional states can be affected. The experiences of others may also provide you with specific strategies for changing emotions of your own that you presently don't know how to change. We recommend that you think of several examples of emotional state changes that you have witnessed in friends and acquaintances, and find out from them what they do to make their emotional choices possible. (They may never have considered what they do until you ask them, so you may need to help them figure it out.)

Having become acquainted with some ways that you and others have gone about changing emotions, you can then move on to noticing in an ongoing way how you affect your own emotional experience. The goal is to be aware of when you have shifted your emotions and to notice just what you did, both inside and outside, to make that change. In this way you will be continually teaching yourself, honing your understanding of the processes involved, and building an invaluable cache of personally affecting strategies.

This chapter deals with providing the informational and experiential foundation you need to actually exercise emotional choice. Here is a format for effectively tapping your emotions, using your fund of information and experience.

1. Specify how you want to feel. (This information may come from the results of one of the three selection formats in the previous chapter.)
2. Ask yourself, "What could I do here and now (or there and then) to get to that emotion?"
3. By searching through your personal history, identify ways that have worked before for you or an acquaintance to access the emotion you have selected.
4. Select the means that seems most appropriate.
5. Do it. If the result is not satisfying, cycle back through steps 3 and 4 and select another means of accessing the emotion.

As you can see, this is about as straightforward an approach as one could imagine. Your current personal resources with respect to accessing emotions are richer and vaster than you suppose, and will increase dramatically if you follow the previous suggestions for gleaning from yourself and others various ways of tapping certain emotions. There is no reason to take a more involved approach if you already have the means of directly accessing the feeling you are after. A point to remember, though, is that once you realize you do have a choice you still must *act* to make that choice real in your experience.

Leslie uses the format for tapping an emotion as an innoculation against boredom. As soon as she begins to feel disengaged, before she has the chance to slip into the doldrums of boredom, she taps into curiosity and fascination by asking herself questions about the people nearby: "What is that person thinking and feeling?" "What's going on in her life?" "How is it possible that that couple isn't talking to each other?" If she is alone, without other people to observe directly, Leslie searches for an item close at hand and asks questions like, "Who made this?" "Why did they design it this way?" "What do they think makes it pretty?" "Did they intend to convey the image or communication that I am receiving right now?"

On more than one occasion, we have turned an otherwise dull restaurant meal into an interesting and fun experience by observing how groups at other tables are behaving—how close together they sit if they are in a booth, whether or not they touch, who talks most and who listens, how each is responding to the other's tempo of speech and tone of voice, and so on. This redirection of attention and change in involvement leads us to speculate about such questions as "What must be going on inside each one to create that behavior?" "Who's the outsider in that family or group?" "Who's paying the bill, and who's not?"

We also use the format to help our teenage son, Mark, prevail in many of his tribulations. When he wanted to ask a girl out on a date, but didn't know how and so felt stuck and inadequate, we had him create a fantasy in which he tried several different approaches on several different girls. We made sure that he imagined some acceptances *and* some rejections so he could practice responding appropriately to both possibilities. With that kind of experience under his belt, his feeling of inadequacy was replaced with confidence. Another opportunity to use the format came when he tried out for the high school tennis team. Mark knew his chances were slim, but he was having a good time and making new friends so he continued playing each afternoon after school for two weeks. When the day of reckoning arrived and he received his pink slip, even though he knew he didn't have a good chance of making the team, he was still disappointed. We helped him move from disappointment to determination by simply changing the criteria and time frame he was using, redirecting his thinking and attention to what he was going to do to be sure to make the team next year.

While some people find it quite easy to adjust their perceptions and behavior in order to change their feelings, you may be one of those who finds it difficult. The harder it is for you to alter your experience and behavior, the more important gaining that ability becomes. Your difficulty in altering your experience and behavior indicates a lack of flexibility that has undoubtedly undermined your desire for emotional choice in the past. The more energy you put into discovering, trying, and experimenting with ways of changing your emotions, the more you will be weighting the scales in favor of flexibility and choice.

## *Self-Anchoring*

*Anchoring* is the technique of pairing some stimulus over which you have control with the emotional state to which you would like to have access. All of us already have many unintentional, yet compelling, anchors to which we automatically respond. For instance, there is the melody that instantly whirls you back to a special evening, or the scent that rekindles in you the feelings you had for a certain person, or the gentle embrace that immediately elicits a sense of safety and acceptance. Each of these "events"—the music, the scent, the embrace—is an anchor for the memories and feelings with which that event was associated.

When creating emotional choice for yourself in a particular situation, you must be able to identify the contextually appropriate emotion and to access that emotion when you need it. For instance, you may need and want to feel curious in class, but can't seem to access that feeling when you are actually sitting in the classroom. Obviously, you need some way of bringing the feeling of curiosity into your current experience. The format for tapping your emotions is one method you can use, but another very effective way of doing this is by establishing an *anchor* that you can use to access the feeling you want to have. When you are in class, feeling bored but wanting and needing to be responsive, you can use your anchor to access feelings of curiosity.

Jonelle, a friend of ours, used anchoring to help her overcome her fear of making a speech. She was petrified at the thought of standing in the glare of all of those hostile eyes. When she confessed her fears to Leslie, who is an experienced seminar speaker, Leslie explained to her that the audience actually wanted her to do well. This revelation was immediately reassuring for Jonelle, but she was worried that her feeling of reassurance would fade when she actually stood before the audience. In order to have access to that reassurance when she needed it, Jonelle made the feeling as intense as she could, then grasped the table top as though it were a lectern. She did this several times, until just by grasping the tabletop she could feel the sense of reassurance welling up inside her. When it came time for the actual speech, she stepped nervously up to the stage. But as soon as she grasped the edge of the lectern, her nervousness melted away, to be replaced by the reassurance that all those people out there were rooting for her.

Jonelle used anchoring to give herself access to the feeling of reassurance when she needed it. The anchor that she used was grasping the top of the lectern—an excellent choice, since that would be precisely when she would need that feeling of reassurance—and she made sure that a lectern would be there. Reassurance is not the only emotion you can access using an anchor. You can use anchoring to give you timely access to any emotion.

Here is a format for the technique of self-anchoring.

1. Identify the feeling you want to have.

2. Remember a time when you experienced that emotion fully. When you have identified the memory, clasp your hands together lightly (or use any other discreet touch signal, such as holding your earlobe between your thumb and forefinger, or touching the side of your nose).

3. Step back into that memory, seeing what you saw, hearing what you heard, and, most important, feeling what you felt then.

4. Once you have immersed yourself in the desired emotion, gently increase the pressure of your clasp or touch as you continue feeling the emotion fully. This action establishes the clasping of your hands, or other touch signal, as the anchor for the feeling.

5. Maintaining the pressure of your touch, reorient yourself to your present surroundings, bringing the emotion with you. If upon reorienting yourself to the present, the emotion subsides, go back through steps 3 and 4 and reaccess the memory and reanchor.

6. Release your hands and enjoy how you feel. If the feeling subsides, perform your touch signal again to reaccess the emotion. Do this until you can both access the emotion using your anchor, and maintain it for a while after you release the anchor.

7. Later, test your anchor by once again pressing your hands together, or touching in the particular way you have decided on. If the anchor does not access the desired emotion, go back through the technique, being sure to intensify the memory as strongly as possible, and adding other memories if necessary.

The heart of this technique is that you steep yourself in a specific emotion, using intense past experiences, then set up a touch signal capable of immediately taking you back to that same feeling. So if you want to have access to feeling amorous, you might go back to memories of feeling particularly passionate, and then anchor them. Or you might want to have access to feeling peaceful, and so remember a time when all seemed especially calm in your life. Or you might recall an experience of relentlessly plugging your way to a finish line, from which to extract feeling determined.

This technique makes it possible for you to anchor particular emotions so that you can have access to them *when you need them*. Obviously, used in this way, anchoring is something you do before you will need the emotions.

For instance, a client of ours named Roy considered himself socially inept. He rarely accepted an invitation to a party, for they always turned out to be opportunities for him to rediscover just how isolated from other people he really felt. Having learned about anchoring, Roy decided to give it a try and accepted an invitation to a get-together in his apartment building. He decided that in order to interact the way he would like to, what he needed to feel was friendly. There were certain people toward whom he felt very friendly. He conjured these people up in his imagination, intensified the feeling of friendliness, then clasped his hands together to anchor the emotion. He repeated this process until merely clasping his hands together filled him with a feeling of friendliness. At the party, Roy's anchor served him well. He had to use it several times early in the evening, but as the other people began reacting to his friendly behavior, his feeling of friendliness became a natural response to the interactions he was enjoying, and so the anchor was no longer needed.

Your own anchor need not be the clasping of hands suggested here. Any distinctive touch will do. For instance, pressing your thumb to your ring finger, or encircling your left wrist with the fingers of your right hand, are distinctive and unusual touches that would be good choices for anchors, as was Jonelle's anchor choice of grasping the top of the lectern. On the other hand, if you commonly clasp your hands together or rub the back of your neck, these would be poor choices for anchors. They would be poor choices because you might inadvertently anchor some other emotion to the same touch, masking or even washing out completely the one you originally anchored. Also, if you are anchoring several emotions intended for use in different situations, you will need to establish separate anchors for each of those emotions.

How well an anchor works depends largely upon how strong it is. When first creating an anchor for an emotion, make your experience of being back in the situation in which you previously felt that emotion as vivid and as compelling as possible. You can increase the strength of the experience by increasing the intensity of your picture's color, brightness, movement, the volume and tempo of what you hear, and the sensations you feel. You can also increase the strength of an anchor by reanchoring the emotion several times, as Jonelle and Roy did. Making the emotion sufficiently intense sometimes involves finding a particularly compelling moment in your past that still affects you deeply when you recall it. For instance, if you want to anchor feelings of love toward your spouse, rather than intensifying the feeling of love you experience now, you might take yourself back to those blood-surging days when you were first attracted to that person.*

## *Breaking Cause-Effects*

Sometimes you may find yourself in an emotional state caused by a situation that is so overwhelming that you are cut off from your usual abilities to change how you feel. At such times, what is going on holds such sway over you that you are unable to change the perceptual components, or engage in the behaviors, that make up the emotional choice strategy that ordinarily works well for you. At such times even the anchors that you have previously set up may be unable to overcome the potency of the situation you are in.

We are talking about those situations in which a particular identifiable stimulus causes you to feel something you do not want to feel. (In fact, many people assume that *all* of their emotions are the result of the various stimuli occurring around them, and therefore try to control how they feel by trying to control the environment—a strategy bound to fail.) Such situations might include the searing anger you feel when Uncle Joe gets on his racist soapbox, or feeling overcome with sadness when you listen to the world news, or being yelled at, or feeling anxious when you receive an audit notice from the IRS. In such situations you are being *controlled*, without choice, by the stimulus of Uncle Joe, the news, the volume and tone of voice, or the IRS.

When this occurs, the best choice is to do something to *break the cause-effect*—that is, to initially nullify the control the stimulus has over you. Once the cause-effect has been broken, you can then, if necessary, shift to the During selection format as a means of regaining choice about your emotions. Breaking the cause-effect has the double virtue of freeing you from the situation's influence enough to shake the unpleasant and inappropriate emotions you have been enduring, and of providing you with an op-

* An in-depth presentation of the technique of anchoring and its uses can be found in *Solutions: Practical and Effective Antidotes for Sexual and Relationship Problems*, by Leslie Cameron-Bandler.

portunity to marshal your perceptual and behavioral resources so that you can reenter the situation on your own terms.

There are three ways to nullify the controlling effect of a stimulus, all of which involve removing yourself in some way from what is going on around you. The first of these ways is to change your perspective to one that is detached from the ongoing situation. You can do this either by viewing the situation from the perspective of some point in the future—so that you are looking back on what was happening—or by visually stepping outside of the situation, watching it from the perspective of an unconnected outside observer, much as you might watch a television show.

A second way to nullify the effect of a controlling stimulus is to shift your attention to another stimulus. For instance, if you were feeling numbingly bored at a lecture you could intentionally turn your attention to an attractive person in the audience, or to something about the room that is strange enough to elicit your curiosity—in short, any stimulus that is compelling enough to elicit a different emotion in you. Akin to this means of breaking cause-effects is to ask questions that lead you to process information. If at a moment when you are overwhelmed by an emotion, you begin to ask yourself questions that have to do with problem-solving, the usual result is to remove you emotionally from the effects of the stimulus. For instance, to nullify the infuriating effects of Uncle Joe's racism, you could pose such questions to yourself as, "How did he come to think this way?" Or, "How did I come to think as I do?" Or, "What could I do that would change what he is doing?"

A third way is physically to leave the situation. If a stimulus is robbing you of the ability to choose how you feel, there is no need to "tough it out." There is a great deal of difference between *running away* and *leaving.* It may be that you will have to remove yourself physically from the stimulus in order to be able to regain choice about your emotions. For example, in Chapter 7, Leslie found it necessary to walk outside of the restaurant to think about what she wanted for herself emotionally and to access those feelings. Once she again had a choice about her feelings, she was ready to return to the restaurant, this time on her own emotional terms. Here are some examples of the kinds of things you can do to remove yourself from paralyzing, overwhelming situations.

□ Someone's whiny and grating speaking voice is causing you to be irritable and short-tempered.

–Shift all of your attention to the other people present.

–Try to figure out what patterns of muscle tension are required to generate such hideous tonality.

–Mimic the tonality.

–Pretend that the tonality is a symptom of a fatal disease.

–Leave.

–Dominate the interaction with your own voice.

□ You are staying with a friend whose apartment is unutterably messy, making you feel disgusted and disagreeable.

–Clean the apartment.

–Make yourself one small, neat area that you can call your own.

–Leave.

–Turn off the lights.

–View it as a deliberate work of art.

–Try to figure out what events led to the deposition of each layer of the mess.

□ You are being ignored by a group, making you feel humiliated and resentful.

–Leave.

–Make a scene.

–Whisper in someone's ear.

–Enjoy being invisible, watching the amusing ways in which people behave.

–Eavesdrop and think of how to later use what you are hearing.

–Take someone aside and engage that one person in conversation.

These examples are offered to stimulate your thinking about the range of possibilities open to you for simply interrupting a situation that is causing you to respond in an inappropriate and resourceless way. It will be worth your while now to select several recent examples of your own of being overwhelmed by a situation, causing you to feel and behave in ways that you did not like. Then generate a list of possible things you could have done at the time to remove yourself from the situation. Once you are familiar with the process of generating those kinds of alternatives, you can use the following format the next time you find yourself in an emotionally overwhelming situation.

1. Identify what is making you feel an emotion that is unpleasant or inappropriate (that is, identify the cause).
2. Select a way to nullify the effect of that cause by either (a) Changing your perspective to being in the future looking back, or to being an outside observer, or (b) Shifting your attention to another stimulus, or (c) Physically removing yourself.
3. Remove yourself in the way that you have selected. If you still feel overwhelmed, go back to step 2 and select another, perhaps more dramatic way to nullify the cause-effect.
4. If you wish, once you have nullified the effect of the stimulus you can move to the During format and to other accessing approaches.

It may be that the relief you get by removing yourself from the cause of the situation is enough for you to feel satisfied. In that case, you can stop with step 3. Before moving on to other things, however, take a moment to consider whether you would eventually like to be able to be in such a situation and not have that cause compel your experience in the way that it has. If you would like that for yourself, then you should take the opportunity to either move to the During format, changing your emotional response to the ongoing situation, or to the After format, changing your emotional response to that situation the next time you find yourself in it. Whether you take advantage of either of these formats, or simply nullify the cause-effect and move on to other things, the point is to bring the situation under your control, rather than letting the situation continue to control you.

## *Remodeling Your Emotions*

In introducing time frames in Chapter 5 we told you about Stephen, whose young son had pushed him to the brink of fury with his continual interruptions. Then, just as he was about to topple into a rage, "Stephen's imagination suddenly leapt to the future. In that future he saw his son full grown, acting rudely, and being isolated and unhappy as a result. At once the conversation of the moment seemed insignificant. The flame in Stephen's eyes died down to a glow. He knelt beside his son and began to explain to him what it means to be rude and what he needed to do to keep from being rude." Although he had not intended it, Stephen had changed his emotional state in a very sophisticated way, by making a crucial change from operating in the present to a future time frame. The moment he changed the time-frame component, his emotion shifted from impatience to patience.

Also in Chapter 5 we told you about Frances and her confrontation with the bank. She failed in her intention to force the bank to rectify its error, and felt completely dissatisfied with herself. But when her friend urged her to find *something* that she had done well in the confrontation, Frances remembered, "Even though I was scared, I told them, 'You haven't heard the last of me,' and walked out." Once Frances recognized her small success, she felt satisfied.

Like Frances, most of us feel dissatisfied when things aren't just the way we want them to be. In order to feel satisfied, Frances had to focus her attention on what she *did* do that fulfilled her expectations. She was unable to do that until she began breaking the incident down into smaller and smaller pieces of behavior (chunking down), finally getting to those behaviors/outcomes that she *did* fulfill in a way that was satisfying to her.

Sometimes you may need to gain access to an emotion component by component, as Stephen and Frances did, rather than stepping into it all at once, which is the outcome of the "Tapping" and "Self-anchoring" formats. You may be so locked into an emotional state that it is not possible to leap from where you are to the emotional state you desire. It's good to have several means of changing your emotional experience, and one of the best approaches is to change your feelings by altering your perceptions at the component level.

Remodeling an emotion into one that is more appropriate involves, first of all, becoming aware of those components that are significant in creating the emotion. One of the easiest ways to identify the components of an emotion is to ask and answer the question, "How would I know if I were feeling that emotion?" Once you know what the components are, you can begin to experiment with changing them. You already know from the examples in previous chapters that the components underlying a particular emotion form a unique set of mutually affecting perceptions. Change any one of those components and your feelings will immediately change as well. In addition, changes in some of those components will have a more profound effect on changing a particular emotion than will changes in other components.

We are not suggesting that you change some aspect of your internal experience simply for the sake of changing your emotion to something—"anything"—else. You probably have some idea of what you would rather be feeling in place of what you are currently saddled with. Where you want to go with your emotional state should serve as a yardstick with which you can measure the quality of your experience as you go about changing it. As you readjust your perceptions, consider the question, "Is this what I want to be feeling, and if it isn't, what qualities am I still missing?" Knowing where you want to go emotionally makes it possible for you to keep adjusting your perceptions until you attain the emotion you are after.

For example, suppose that you are feeling impatient and you would like to feel patient. As you become aware of your internal experience you realize that your tempo is quite fast. You also realize that you are keeping your goal in the very near future, and that the modality is one of necessity ("I must have that!"). Experimenting, you start by slowing down your tempo. This changes your emotional state, but not in the way you want. Now you need to attain your goal quickly while operating at a slow tempo, which makes you feel inadequate. So you resume experimenting, this time moving your outcome further into the future. This change, combined with the slowed tempo, does lead you to feel patient.

In fact, you can experience any emotion whose set of

components you can describe. This may seem a more sophisticated and challenging approach to accessing emotions, but after just a few tries it becomes easy. The payoff of using this method goes beyond gaining access to specific emotions; it also provides you with an orientation and a growing fund of information that will make your ongoing experience and the emotional responses of others a continuing source of new knowledge regarding the structure of human experience. And with that knowledge will come a level of choice and a range of emotional experience that is not otherwise possible.

The following examples, which will give you a rich sense of the emotion remodeling process, are common ones. That is, the component changes needed to remodel an unwanted emotion into a particular desired one are those that most people need to make in order to have access to that desired emotion. As you read each example, access each of the components described and discover how your feelings change. If you do not feel the emotion that that set of components is intended to create, consider what is missing and try adding that additional perception into the set.

## *Inadequate to Adequate*

*You have agreed to speak on a panel, but when you discover that all of the other panel members have more academic degrees than you do, you feel inadequate.* Often, the most significant component in generating the feeling of inadequacy is that of making a comparison between what you have or can do and what some other person has or can do. You can change this to a feeling of adequacy by reminding yourself of your own capabilities, past demonstrations of unique competence, and so on, until you feel that you are capable of holding your own with that other person—or, in the case of our example, that you are adequate to act as a member of the panel.

## *Overwhelmed to Responsibly Creative*

*Although it has been quite an undertaking, you have managed to get everything ready for your child's birthday party. But when it turns out that twice as many children show up as you had expected, you feel completely overwhelmed.* When you feel overwhelmed your tempo is rapid as you try to take care of too many tasks at once, without setting priorities. You can generate a feeling of responsible creativity by making three changes. First, slow down your tempo, and then set priorities and sequences for the tasks you are facing. You are chunking down this overwhelming task into the various smaller tasks that make it up, then concentrating only on what needs to be done first. When that is done, you move on to the next task—for instance, first get the young guests occupied doing something, then figure out what additional food is needed, find someone to go get it, etc. Second, to the criterion "getting it all done," add "having fun." At the same time, change the modality from "I must/I have to" to "I want to/I can." The combination of these changes will result in your coming up with ideas for activities and treats—group games outdoors, making peanut butter goo balls, baking cookies—that are fun for you and for the kids and at the same time solve problems such as a shortage of food.

### *Anxious to Capable*

*It is Saturday evening and you are sitting at your desk wringing your hands with anxiety because on Monday you are facing a final exam that will make or break your grade in the class.* Anxiety is often generated when you are facing a future that seems to hold danger, and for which you are unprepared. You can turn this into a feeling of being capable first by attending only to what is going on right now until you feel safe in the present. ("The house is warm and comfortable, I've got my favorite books and pictures around me, I have friends, people who love me.") Then adopt a modality of "it is possible" and begin to chunk down by thinking of ways that you could usefully prepare yourself to tackle that possibly dangerous future. ("First I need to get out my notes and figure out what is likely to be on the test, then I'll study that first, then, if I still have time, I can go on to study other things that might be on the test.")

### *Disappointment to Frustration*

*An employee for whom you had high expectations and big plans has disappointed you by demonstrating that he is unable to fulfill those expectations and plans.* When you are expecting something you really want and you don't get it, the result may be disappointment. The significant component here is that you are no longer imagining the *possibility* of getting what you want. By putting what you want into a continuing time frame that extends into the future (for instance, telling yourself that your employee hasn't measured up *yet*), you will at least move to feeling frustrated. This is a useful move in this case because frustration tends to keep you engaged in the pursuit of your outcomes, such as continuing to try to educate your employee so that he can eventually attain the level you believe he is capable of achieving. If you want to move from frustration to the more pleasurable anticipation, identify times in the past when your employee learned and improved. Using those examples as reassurance, keep using a future time frame but change your modality from "he might change" to "he will change." This will allow you to make pictures of a future worth anticipating. It might also infuse you with a renewed sense of enthusiasm and excitement.

### *Disappointment to Acceptance*

*Your teenager leaves to get her split ends and bangs trimmed, and four hours later returns with a green-tinged punk hairdo.* You may not want or be able to continue to pursue an outcome that you have been disappointed in getting. In that case, you may want to move from disappointment to acceptance, freeing you to move on to other outcomes. You can do this by moving into the future a few years and then looking back on what it was that you didn't get. As you look back at the outcome that you didn't get, make it perceptually smaller and smaller, less and less consequential, until you feel acceptance. For example, looking back on your daughter's garish hairdo from the perspective of ten years in the future, it becomes just one of those curious and amusing incidents in the life of a teenager.

### *Depressed to Encouraged*

*You feel that you are not doing anything worthwhile and you can't see that you ever really have; and when you look into the future, all you can see is a lot more of the same, meaningless going-through-the-motions . . . and it's so depressing.* When you are feeling depressed, the past, present, and future all look bad. To pull yourself out of depression you need to begin by identifying *something* that is better now than it once was. Build that small difference into the future, then find another something that is now better and build that into the future, and so on. In this way you will eventually build a future that will dispel your depression and nurture a feeling of encouragement. However, your feeling of depression probably won't change to encouragement immediately. You should view the process as being akin to raising a heavy object from the ocean floor by pumping more and more bubbles of air into that object.

## *Hopeful to Responsible*

*You find out that your six-year-old son has been stealing small items, and you certainly hope that he changes this very damaging habit.* When there is something you want, but your orientation toward that outcome is *passive,* you are likely to remain hopeful of getting what you want without necessarily doing anything to get it. If instead you felt responsible, you would be much more likely to become engaged in trying to do something about attaining the outcome. In this case, feeling responsible for your child's future would engage you in teaching him to respect other people's property. You can reorient yourself to feeling responsible by altering the internal "I wish it would happen" to "It must be done" and "I am the one who must do it," (modality of necessity), by reminding yourself of other parenting outcomes you have accomplished so that you generate "I *can* do what must be done," and then by beginning to consider ways to fulfill your outcome.

## *Bored to Pleasurable Anticipation*

*You are on a long automobile trip through territory that holds no interest or attraction for you, and you feel bored.* When you are bored you are in the present, but nothing of interest is going on in that present. You can remodel the feeling of boredom into either pleasure or pleasant anticipation by shifting your attention to the future and fantasizing about positive future possibilities. In the case of the car trip, you could transport yourself in your imagination to the pleasing things that await you at the end of your journey.

## *Grief to Acceptance*

*You have lost a loved one, someone whose future was intertwined with your own, and now you are grieving.* In addition to the death of a loved one, you might also feel grief over the loss of a job, a house, a dream, or a relationship. In fact, because we tend to associate grief with death, many people do not recognize that they are grieving over the loss of something else, such as a relationship or a job. When you are grieving you continue to compare what is *not* here in your present with what *could* be here, and what will *not* be there in your future with what that future *could have been*. In order to move to acceptance, you need to build a near and a continuing future, beginning with the present, made up of what *will* be there that will be satisfying, what you *will be doing* that will be satisfying, and how you *will* do it. You will then be attending to *one* future, rather than comparing the two futures of "what will be" with "what could have been."

## *Satisfied to Thrilled*

*Your seven-year-old daughter comes home with a sheet of addition and subtraction problems, all of which she has solved correctly, and you feel satisfied with her progress.* Satisfaction is what you feel when what is happening is just what you had wanted to happen. The intensity of this emotion is generally not very high. If you are only feeling satisfied with a situation that warrants much more juice (such as your daughter being able to add and subtract), you can crank up the intensity of your feeling of satisfaction—perhaps by using this event as evidence of a future of accomplishment, greatness, and fulfillment for your child—until you are feeling thrilled.

Take yourself through the examples we have just described, repeat them a few times, and you will discover that you will soon integrate them as strategies of your own, giving you new emotional choices in contexts that have in the past been troublesome for you.

The following exercise will provide you with the opportunity to experience and experiment with the remodeling of emotions of your own selection.

1. Identify an emotion that you are experiencing. (For instance, "I'm feeling curious.")
2. Identify the significant components of the emotion by asking yourself, "How do I know I'm feeling ___*(the emotion)*___ as compared to any other emotion?" That is, as you consider the time frame, tempo, modality,

degree of involvement, intensity, matching/mismatching/comparing, criteria, and chunk size, what seems to stand out as significant in making that emotion what it is? (For instance, "When I'm feeling curious, I notice a mismatch between what I know and what is being presented to me, I'm concerned with the present, I feel intensely involved, and my criterion is one of 'understanding.' The mismatching, criterion of 'understanding,' and intense involvement seem most significant to me.")

3. Change one of the significant components in some qualitative or quantitative way. If you are attending to the present, you could instead attend to the past or future. If your tempo is fast, slow it down; or if it is slow, speed it up. If your modality is one of necessity ("I must," "I have to"), change it to possibility ("I could," "I might"); or change it from possibility to necessity. If the degree of involvement that you feel is active, change to feeling passive; or, if passive, change to feeling active. You can either increase or decrease the intensity of what you are feeling. If you are attending to how things match, change to attending to how they mismatch or compare. You can change the criterion—that is, what is important to you in the situation—to some other criterion. Or you can keep the criterion the same but either chunk up or down from how you are currently viewing it.

4. Notice how your emotions change as a result of the changes you make in the components of your experience. (For instance, "When I start matching I no longer feel curious, but *motivated* to do something. When I reduce intensity my feeling of curiosity fades to *interested*, and when I increase intensity I feel *burningly curious*. When I shift to feeling passive, I feel *interested*.")

We encourage you to repeat the above exercise often, with as diverse a set of emotions and components as you can find. The exercise may seem simple, but it is nevertheless a superb education in the structure of subjective experience. This kind of experimentation is invaluable to you in learning to appreciate and become facile with the internal processes that generate your ongoing emotions. In fact, it is a fundamental aspect of true emotional choice.

Here is an especially helpful tip for quickly accessing an emotion. It will help you access different emotions to use in the above exercise. The tip is in the form of a question, and we have altered people's emotions thousands of times by asking it. We have used the question when they have wanted to feel a certain emotion, or when we wanted them to feel the emotion. Let's use ambition as an example. The question is this: "How would you know if you were feeling ambitious?" In order to answer, the person needs to access the emotion before he or she can make the evaluation required to describe the components. You can use the question on yourself. Any time you want to access a particular emotion, ask yourself, "How would I know if I were feeling ambitious?" (or appreciative, or determined, etc.). When you begin to experience the emotion, you can anchor it if you want.

Once you have gained facility with modeling the components of emotions, you can use the following four-step format to remodel your emotional states to suit your desires. The four steps parallel the stages that have been discussed and referred to throughout this section.

1. Become aware of the significant components underlying an unwanted emotion.
2. Change the qualities of those components, one at a time.
3. Evaluate whether that change leads you toward attaining the emotion you want to have.
4. Continue to change significant components of the unwanted emotion until you have attained the emotion you desire.

Three final points need to be made about remodeling your emotions. The first regards the length of the emotional leap you take. If you are feeling fatigued, it may be too long a jump to feeling vital or ambitious. If your goal is too distant to be made in one emotional jump, take it in increments, hopping from one easily accessible emotion to the next. For instance, you might go from feeling fatigued to feeling bored to feeling restless to feeling motivated to feeling ambitious. Notice how these emotions are structurally closer to one another and more accessible, allowing you to step easily from one to another.

The second point concerns the time involved in remodeling

an emotion. When remodeling, you sometimes need to apply an extended time frame to your progress. While you will often be able to remodel your emotions in a matter of seconds, other emotional changes could take hours or days to change—depression, for instance. Still other emotions, such as grief, may take weeks. Building internal images of a new future that is satisfying—one of the changes that needs to be made to transform grief into acceptance—may take awhile.

The third point is relevant to all of the accessing approaches presented in this chapter. Presumably you will be using these approaches to give yourself access to certain emotions that you need in particular contexts. (Most of the time you will not actually be *in* the situation while you are figuring out what emotion you wish to access and how to go about it.) It is therefore important that you have a way of ensuring that you are able to access how you want to feel when you want to feel it. We call this process *future-pacing*. Once you have gained access to the emotion you desire, future-pacing allows you to attach it to the context in which you need it.

Future-pacing is done by imagining as vividly as possible the next situation in which you will need this newly acquired emotional response. Step into that imagined situation *with the desired emotion*, and feel what you will feel, see what you will see, and hear what you will hear. (This is also an excellent opportunity to establish for that emotion an anchor that you can use as backup or reinforcement when you later actually find yourself in the situation.) Besides providing a final check that the emotion you have acquired is what you want in that situation, future-pacing helps to ensure that you have access to that emotion when you need it, so that you will not need to repeat either the selection or the accessing formats.*

## *What You Have Now*

Having choice is more than knowing what you want, and it's more than picking something worth having. All of us have

* Leslie Cameron-Bandler's book *Solutions: Practical and Effective Antidotes for Sexual and Relationship Problems* contains a discussion and several demonstrations of the use of future-pacing.

wandered the aisles of the emotional toy store, wanting this, aching for that, in the end walking out empty-handed because we lacked the currency we needed to get what we wanted. Having emotional choice means selecting well *and* having a way to make that selection a reality.

This chapter has introduced effective means of accessing or acquiring the emotions you choose. These approaches included *Tapping Emotions*, in which you use your own naturally occurring ways of accessing certain emotions; *Self-Anchoring*, in which you create physical signals that allow you to access the emotions you want, when you want them; *Breaking Cause-Effects*, in which you gain access to your emotional resources by first separating yourself from the emotionally overwhelming situation; and *Remodeling Emotions*, in which you discover the significant components within a desired emotion and then alter your perceptions to match.

Learning to access emotions is what will make your selections of emotions come true; it is the fulfillment of the choice. The ability of Placement—the ability to orient to, select, and access emotions—can mean a new range of choice and tremendous effectiveness for you in securing both your short- and long-term outcomes. Like so many things that are worth doing, the formats we have described here do take some time and energy to master, but it is an investment in an ever-expanding future of emotional and behavioral possibilities.

9

# *Expressing Your Emotions*

WHENEVER OUR FRIEND BARRY WAS FEELING ANGRY, frustrated, confused, tired, ambitious, disappointed, serene, or satisfied, his behavior was the same—he shut himself up in his den, pecking away at the keyboard of his computer, staring into the green glow of the monitor. Shut off from him in this way, Barry's family could only speculate about his mood. Erring on the side of caution and concern, they assumed the worst, leaving him alone and hoping that his "terrible" mood would pass. Eventually they learned to live without him.

Whenever Laura was feeling angry, frustrated, confused, tired, disappointed, lonely, nostalgic, or anxious, she cried. It wasn't long before no one cared about her tears. Those around her could do nothing but sigh, "There she goes again. Oh well, she'll get over it soon enough," and then go on about their business.

For the most part, other people know what is going on inside you by observing your behavior. Of course, as we illustrated above with a couple of extreme (though actual) examples, what they "know" about your emotional state may be incorrect. The behavioral expressions for the emotions that Barry and Laura have available to them are so limited and inappropriate that it's no wonder their families and friends are forever misreading their moods. To some extent, the problem of appropriate emotional expression is one that we all share. All of us can come up with personal examples of emotions that we express in clumsy, detrimental, or misleading ways.

The expression of emotions need not be determined by default. You can choose not only your emotions, but how to express them as well. By having choices about emotional expression, you will enhance your effectiveness in attaining outcomes and communicating with others, as well as enhancing your experience of yourself. It is through the expression of our emotions that we manifest ourselves as feeling beings.

In the previous three chapters you learned the skills behind Placement, the first key ability of emotional choice. In this chapter you will learn the second key ability, Expression, by learning a format that guides you through the selection of behaviors that are expressive of the emotion you are feeling, congruent with your self, and appropriate for the circumstances in which you find yourself.

Typically, people have very little flexibility when it comes to expressing their emotions. For the most part, we seem to be confined to expressing our emotions the way we have always expressed them, even if that expression has proved unfulfilling and ineffective. By using the format presented in this chapter, you will greatly expand your repertoire of expressive behaviors. In addition, you will come to better recognize just what your desired outcome is in a given situation, how your emotions can aid you in this recognition, and how to most effectively secure that outcome through the appropriate expression of your emotions.

## *To Express or Not to Express?*

Most of us seem to keep our concept of self, our emotions, and our behavioral expression all within the same conceptual "box":

| | | |
|---|---|---|
| | *who I am* | (concept of self) |
| ME = | *what I feel* | (emotions) |
| | *what I do* | (behavioral expression) |

The problem with keeping these three facets of ourselves within the confines of the same box is that when one of the facets seems to be incongruent with the others it can quickly become mighty crowded and uncomfortable in there. This often happens when we feel some emotion that seems to us to be incongruent with our concept of self. You may feel envious of a friend's new romance, which is a violation of your concept of your self, and consequently consider yourself "bad" for feeling that way. Furthermore, you will probably then do anything *but* express that emotion, for to do so would be to reveal to others your "badness."

There seems to be a certain set of emotions that are considered wrong or bad to feel, let alone express, in our culture. These include feeling horny, confused, irritated, curious (about other people's business), irresponsible, haughty, and envious. Of course, all of us do feel these emotions from time to time. But when we do, we often assume that they must not be expressed. The most common next step is to consider the emotion as evidence of badness, weakness, egotism, depravity, or childishness, which often leads to feelings of shame.

For example, Martha works for a man who obviously has high standards and definite ideas about how things should be done, but who rarely tells her explicitly what those standards and ways are. This leaves Martha feeling confused, with many questions about her tasks at the office. Part of Martha's self-concept is that she should already know how to do things, and so, to her, her feelings of confusion mean that she is dumb. In order not to expose her "dumbness" to her boss, Martha never asks him any questions, which leads her again and again to do her job in a way that her boss considers incompetent. A few more laps around this circle of quicksand and Martha's job won't just be confusing, it will be history.

The real problem here is that Martha is using her *emotions* as evidence of the fulfillment of self-concept, rather than using her *behavior* as that evidence. One of the wonderful things about your emotions is that they provide you with ongoing feedback about what is going on with you, and they should be regarded in that way. For example, feeling sullen and acting sullen are two very different things—as we pointed out in Chapter 2, you could be acting in a sullen fashion while not feeling that way at all. Once you think of your emotions as ongoing feedback about what is going on with you, you are immediately promoted from the experiential back seat, where you are merely along for the emotional ride, to the driver's seat, where you can make decisions about where you want your experience to go.

One of the first decisions you can freely make from the driver's seat is whether or not to express a particular emotion. When people decide to *not* express an emotion it is usually because they either have no way of expressing it that is appropriate to the situation, or they consider their way of expressing it to be incongruent with their concept of self. You may be feeling amorous, but only know how to express that emotion in a way that your lover finds crass and crude, and so you decide to not express it at all. Or you may be feeling amorous, but believe the way you know to express that emotion to be incongruent with who you are and how you want to be perceived by your lover. In either case, what you need is some flexibility in choosing how to express what you are feeling. In this way you will be deciding whether or not to express an emotion on the basis of whether you want and need to, rather than on the basis of whether the emotion is "bad" or whether you have the ability to express it well.

There are several distinct problems with not expressing emotions. The first is that what is going on inside you fails to be conveyed to those around you. You have a message, but it stays locked inside. But, as with the man in the iron mask, being locked away does not blunt the need and desire to be free. For instance, many people allow their feelings of irritation to go unexpressed for long periods of time. The feeling of irritation does not meekly surrender and disperse, however. Instead, it builds and builds until it finally erupts as intense anger, which *is* expressed. Those caught in the path of the eruption are left wondering where in the world all *that* suddenly came from?

A second problem with allowing emotions to go unexpressed is that by doing so you rob yourself of an opportunity to get what you want. You feel irritated when some small, repetitious thing is going on that you don't like. If you don't express your irritation, the person who is performing the irritating action will not know that she is bothering you and therefore doesn't have the opportunity to change her behavior in order to relieve your irritation. Similarly, when you are feeling amorous, if you don't express your feelings to your lover you may miss an opportunity to discover that he or she is feeling the same way, or would like to feel that way. (Ah, the little benefits of emotional choice: "So, dear, how would you know if you *were* feeling amorous?")

This same situation can easily degenerate into feelings of resentment. When you want something from others, such as attention, affection, respect, solitude, or a breather, but do not express that want to them, the result is often that you feel dissatisfied—because, of course, the people around you don't know what you want of them, and so probably don't do what you want them to do. Usually this dissatisfaction leads to resentment, even though you never actually told anyone what you wanted them to do. Resentment is almost always the result of not expressing an emotion.

Third, not expressing your emotions is bad for your health. We have all felt the body tension created by not expressing something that we really would like to express. The bookshelves, medical and psychological journals, and almost everyone's personal experiences as well, are filled with examples.

And fourth, people can't know who you are if they have no idea what you are feeling. Your emotions are an important aspect of who you are. When you lock them away you are denying your family, colleagues, and friends the opportunity to know and appreciate the depth and range of feeling that is truly *you*.

As you can see, there are ample reasons for expressing your emotions. This does not mean that you should *always* express *all* of your emotions. The first choice to be made is whether or not to express a particular emotion, for there will be times when the expression of certain emotions will be inappropriate, such as feeling joyful while attending a funeral. Perhaps you think that example is farfetched; but that kind of thinking is precisely the pattern that leads to problems. Believe, for a moment, that the deceased person suffered terrible physical and mental pain as his condition deteriorated, and that his death not only brought him relief, but also that he is at last getting to be with departed friends and family whom he has missed for many years, and perhaps you will see how it is possible for a mourner to feel joyful. Still, you may decide that the context is just not appropriate for the *expression* of a certain emotion, at which point it is time to select and access more appropriate emotions, using the formats described in the two previous chapters.

Nevertheless, for the four reasons just given, we want to encourage you to "hang in there" and find a congruent and effective way to express your emotions. It will often happen that you have feelings that you find somehow troublesome and assume that you need to choose another emotion to feel, as described in Chapter 6. But there is usually nothing wrong or inappropriate about what you are feeling—only with how you express that feeling.

## *Choosing Expression*

Being able to choose how you express your emotions is an ability that contributes to fulfilling many goals. Inherent in having greater choice about the expression of your emotions is the possibility of an expanded range of emotions to express, new flexibility in how you respond to various situations, enhanced effectiveness in achieving your outcomes, and a satisfying congruity between your behavioral expressions, the circumstances, and your self-concept.

Your behavior is a natural manifestation of the emotions you are feeling. The naturalness of this connection does not mean, however, that the particular behavior you manifest when feeling a certain way is *the* way that people manifest that emotion, nor does it mean that you cannot learn to manifest that emotion in other ways. The vast majority of emotional expressions that you now manifest you have *learned.* They are now "natural" in the sense of operating automatically. To give you a better idea of what is possible, here are some before and after examples of people who have used the Expression format we will describe to you in a moment.

### *Affection (with friends)*

Before, the only way our trainee Phil had to express his affection was physically (hugging, stroking, kissing), which made some of his friends very uncomfortable. After he learned the format, Phil increased his range of expression to include verbal statements, small gifts, eagerly extending a helping hand, and sending poems and articles of interest to his friends.

### *Anger (with friends and family)*

Bill originally expressed his anger through volume, and sometimes by throwing things around the room. He would then revert to either cruel sarcasm or seething withdrawal. People were afraid of Bill and felt helpless to respond to him usefully. Once Bill could choose, he began to talk about what he was feeling, his reasons for feeling that way, and how he thought the situation should be resolved, rather than constantly blowing up.

### *Sympathy*

Marlene was painfully awkward in expressing the sympathy she felt for those who were suffering emotionally, and either avoided friends in pain or blurted out hollow homilies. Even the people she cared about most deeply thought that she was hard-hearted. Opting for a better form of expression, she now offers her help if it is wanted, gathers information about what is going on in order to find out how she can best help, or quietly remains at her friend's side.

### *Satisfaction*

Whether in her many calls and letters to her friends or when bending the ear of an anonymous bank teller, Donna would express her feelings of personal pride and satisfaction by bragging about her accomplishments. Soon her friends took no delight in Donna's accomplishments, but came to resent her constant bragging. Wanting to maintain the respect and affection of her friends, Donna sought our advice and, as a result, learned to hold more personal celebrations of her accomplishments—as small as going to a movie, or as large as taking a vacation, depending upon how big she feels her accomplishment is. Sometimes she includes friends in the celebration, making it one of mutual pleasure.

### *Ambition*

Our colleague Stephen used to aggressively pursue individuals who he thought could help him in his career, haranguing them with extensive accounts of his ambitions and intentions. Eventually he realized that the people he approached often thought him too pushy. Now Stephen expresses his feelings of ambition by completing projects and generating things to do, and especially by listening for and asking questions about opportunities—that is, by gathering information. The result has been that others now see him as being interested, curious, and as a man with promise.

### *Dissatisfied*

Whenever our client Peter was dissatisfied he would express his feelings by whining and complaining to his friends, family, and associates. People were seldom disposed either to respond to his complaints or to want to stay around him. He now either keeps quiet until he can do something about the source of his dissatisfaction (that is, he chooses not to express his emotion); or he cracks a sarcastic joke, although not at anyone's expense; or he states his dissatisfaction matter-of-factly and asks for assistance.

### *Caution*

When asked for a commitment by those close to her, our friend Katy would either withdraw or, if cornered, would lash out with a barrage of attack-type questions. Katy's flight-or-fight days are over. She now expresses her caution by stating up front that she is not ready to make a commitment, and then begins gathering information that addresses her caution and leads her to feeling more secure.

### *Embarrassment*

Our friend Steve used to withdraw as completely as possible when he felt embarrassed, even if he was with friends. If he could not physically leave the situation, he would pretend he was a piece of furniture. He now exclaims, "Well, that's pretty embarrassing," comes up with some self-parodying remark that he and others find amusing, and then moves the attention of the group elsewhere.

You may not agree with the expressive changes that some of these people made for themselves. You would do it differently, perhaps, because you are a different person, facing your own unique circumstances and possessed of your own unique self-concept. However, these examples do demonstrate first, that there are ways of expressing emotions that are more congruent with your outcomes and self-concept than those you may be using now; and second, that your mode of emotional expression can be changed.

The people in the above examples were able to select new and more useful emotional expressions by taking themselves through the following format. So that you can better follow the steps, we will add an example. Suppose that you are the parent of a teenage son and you have just found out that he is sexually active. You explode, angrily shaking your finger at him as you tell him that he is too young for sex, that he doesn't know what he's doing, that he'll ruin his life and maybe someone else's as well, and so on, until he can't stand it any longer and stomps out of the house. Even though your fears are legitimate, it is immediately obvious that you did not have the impact you wanted to have on your son, so you decide to change how you express yourself in this situation.

1. Identify the emotion that you have been expressing in a way that is unsatisfactory to you. (You are angry, but you realize that what you want to express is not your anger, but your feeling of concern that your son may ruin his own life and that of someone else.)

2. Identify what you want to accomplish through your expression of this emotion. For example, do you want to remain engaged and mobilized? Elicit certain responses from others, and if so, what responses? Simply convey what you are feeling to others? Behave congruently? (Regarding your son's sexuality, you want to instill in him a sense of responsibility and of caution.)

3. Generate at least five possible expressions of this emotion. In doing this you can use your own past experiences and examples of other people's behavior, as well as creating new possibilities. (You could yell at him; buy books for him to read that will educate him about sex; arrange a meeting with a Planned Parenthood counselor; bring over a struggling teenage mother and her children for your son to meet and talk with; have him attend a group counseling session on teenage sexuality and pregnancy; or have a serious discussion with him, explaining the consequences of sexual activity and checking to be sure that he understands them.)

4. For each possibility, run a "movie" in which you see yourself feeling the emotion and expressing it in that way. Decide which possible expression(s) appears most useful, given what you want to accomplish. If none of the possibilities appears useful and appropriate, then cycle back to the previous step and generate other possibilities. (You decide the "serious talk" choice is best, with the counseling group or Planned Parenthood appointment options as something to do if it turns out that your son is unable or unwilling to recognize the responsibilities and consequences involved in his sexual activity.)

5. With the expression(s) you have selected, replay the movie, this time refining your behavior further and checking to make sure that it will indeed lead to the outcomes you desire for that situation. (You imagine having the talk with your son, and arranging an appointment with a Planned Parenthood counselor for reinforcement, and both choices seem worthwhile.)

6. Step into the movie, *feel* the emotion, and imagine as fully as possible how it will be to express it in this way. (By stepping first into having the serious talk with your son, and then into the counseling session, you discover how you will express your concern for your son in these situations.)

7. Identify an upcoming situation in which you are likely to experience the emotion. (Your son has a date tomorrow evening, and you know that as evening approaches you will feel that same concern for him.) Imagine being in that

situation, feeling the emotion, and expressing it in the way you have chosen.

8. Repeat step 7 for at least two other upcoming situations, making minor adjustments in your behavior if necessary. If you discover that there are certain contexts for which your new form of expression is inappropriate, run through the sequence again, beginning with step 2, for that different context.

The first two steps of this format are essential because they have you specify both the emotion you are feeling and the outcome you want to fulfill in the situation. It is important to be aware of both your emotion and your desired outcome so that you can better select a form of expression that is congruent, both with how you are feeling and with what you want to accomplish by making your feelings known. Trying to change your emotionally expressive behavior without knowing what you are feeling and what your outcome is would be like trying to embark on a trip without knowing how you want to travel and where you want to go.

Asking yourself, "What do I want in this situation?" is an equally important step, for the answer to that question will often provide you with the information you need in order to make appropriate changes. For instance, in exploring her frequent feelings of irritation with others, Doris discovered that she wanted others to eat, dress, and raise their children "right." Of course, it was irritating to constantly face examples of people not doing these things "right," and therefore doing them "wrong." When Doris recognized that she always felt irritated with others, she realized that she did not need to change her expression of irritation, but the feeling of irritation itself, to something like curious or accepting.

Once you know where you are and where you want to go, you can begin coming up with ways to get there. This is the function of the third format step, in which you generate at least five possible ways of expressing what you are feeling. The source of these possibilities can be anything that stimulates your thinking regarding how people can express themselves: your own experiences, the experiences of others, movies, books, and so on. In addition, you can (and we recommend that you do) simply speculate about what you might do in order to better express your feelings in the particular situation you are concerned about.

The purpose of steps 4 and 5 is to give you the opportunity to test the appropriateness of the expressions you have chosen. That gem of an expression that appears to shine so brightly by itself may be revealed, when placed in context, as only paste. For example, Barbara felt resentful toward her husband when he acted childishly angry over every little thing that went wrong. She decided that the best way to express herself at those times would be to laugh at him. She was satisfied with her choice until we had her imagine actually doing it. She quickly realized that he might be so outraged by her laughter that he would leave her, or at least be intensely hurt. She decided to generate some other, more useful ways of expressing resentment.

Steps 6, 7, and 8 are intended to help you future-pace the behavioral choice you have made, taking you several times to the situation in which you wish to experience your chosen expression and anchoring it to that situation by having you feel, see, and hear as compellingly as possible just what you will experience when you later do find yourself in that situation, feeling that emotion.

We suggest that you go through this format before you need it. It's too much to ask of yourself to make the necessary evaluations and behavioral adjustments while you are submerged in the emotion and the situation that has triggered it. As surprising as it may seem, it is usually easier to change from one emotion to another than it is to change how you express a particular emotion.

The following example will give you a sense of the use and flow of the Expression format. It is a transcript of a session we had with an executive who found herself repeatedly blowing up at her staff, a practice that was creating a serious gulf between her and them.

**Authors:** You said that you "blow up" at other people, particularly those you work with. What are you feeling when this happens?

**Arlene:** Irritated, but I mean *really* irritated.

**Authors:** OK. What don't you like about how you express irritation now?

**Arlene:** Well, it's just not effective, and a little undignified, I suppose. It really doesn't do any of us any good.

**Authors:** What would you like to achieve by expressing your irritation at those times?

**Arlene:** I want to set limits on the other people—to educate them, really, about how they're irritating me.

**Authors:** OK, what are five possible ways to express irritation, other than what you have been doing? Don't evaluate or censor as you come up with these. Just be as creative as you can.

**Arlene:** Let's see . . . Uh, I could growl, I could rip up papers. I could . . . tell them right away what I am getting irritated about. I could glare at them. That's four . . . I could sigh heavily and meaningfully.

**Authors:** All right, now taking them one at a time, imagine using each of those ways of expressing your irritation and pick out those that are useful in terms of "educating" them. Which are most useful?

**Arlene:** Truly, the only one that's really useful is saying what's irritating me right away, when I first start to get irritated.

**Authors:** Fine. Now let's check that a moment. See yourself in a movie at work, and you can see that you are irritated, but that this time you say right away what you are irritated about. Does that get you what you want in that situation?

**Arlene:** It certainly is a lot less self-indulgent. It's OK. Yeah. Doesn't seem all that difficult.

**Authors:** Keep going through it and refining what you do until it fulfills your outcome and you're satisfied with it.

**Arlene:** OK. I got it.

**Authors:** Great. Now, finally, step into the picture and feel the emotion, your irritation, in that situation and imagine expressing yourself in this new way. . . . Got it?

**Arlene:** Uh huh.

**Authors:** OK. Now think of some upcoming occasion in which you will probably feel the same way . . .

**Arlene:** That's easy.

**Authors:** . . . and step into that situation, feeling irritated and expressing your irritation in this new way you've chosen.

**Arlene:** Much better. Really.
**Authors:** Now pick two other upcoming situations and go through the same process. . . . Got it?
**Arlene:** Got it.

What Arlene "got" was a new way to express herself when she felt irritated, a way that was congruent with who she is and effective in terms of helping her attain her outcome of educating her staff about the things that irritate her. Arlene got one new way to express herself, but you may find that there are some emotions for which you will need several different ways of expressing yourself, depending upon the situation you are in at the time.

Bill, another client of ours, provides an example of needing more than one way to express oneself. The only way that Bill had of expressing his anger was to start yelling, slamming doors, and throwing things around, no matter where he was. What he wanted to accomplish through expressing his anger was to stop or rectify some injustice. In taking himself through the Expression format, he discovered that the means of expression that he came up with took care of one particular situation, but not all situations. Eventually he needed to generate five different ways of expressing his anger for five different contexts. Now, instead of yelling and slamming doors when he is angry, Bill's behavior depends on the context.

In a restaurant where he has been subjected to exceptionally bad service, Bill departs in midmeal, graciously but very publicly, explaining to the host, waiter, and manager his reasons for leaving.

When a contractor has damaged one of Bill's buildings and refuses to take responsibility for it, Bill has his lawyer immediately contact the contractor by phone and letter, giving a deadline for repairs before a suit is filed.

When he finds out that his son has been out drinking after curfew, Bill explains to his son the dangers of this behavior and takes away privileges until his son can demonstrate responsibility in other areas and thus regain his trust.

Discovering that his wife has once again left one of his treasured tools out in the elements (for which she is sorry), he firmly explains how important the tools are to him, what will happen to them if they are left out, and that if she continues to leave them out he will lock them up and she will have to get her own tools.

Discovering a bank error on his business checking account, Bill immediately sets up an appointment with bank officials, at which he demands that letters be sent to his creditors acknowledging the bank's error.

For Bill, each of these contexts was distinct, requiring different expressions of anger. By using the Expression format he was forced to concentrate on what he wanted to have happen in each situation, rather than on what *had* happened in the past. This feature of the format makes it easier to find and adopt new and more satisfying expressions.

## *Incongruity*

There may be situations in which you think that it would be inappropriate to express what is actually going on inside you emotionally. That is, what you are expressing on the outside is not congruent with how you feel on the inside. For instance, suppose that you are leading a child along a dangerous and unfamiliar trail at night, a situation that fills you with a feeling of uncertainty. The child's well-being is in your hands, and even though you feel uncertain, you think that it would be unnecessarily alarming for the child if you congruently expressed your feelings of uncertainty. So you try to project a state of calmness and self-assurance in order to help the child.

As you can see, both how to express an emotion and whether to express it at all are choices that are best made by considering just what your most significant outcomes are for a particular situation. If you are feeling amorous toward a friend's wife and you don't want to jeopardize your present relationship with them, then it is probably best not to express that emotion. Or perhaps you are in a bar being taunted by local thugs. You feel angry and even contemptuous toward them, but unless your desired outcome is to get into a fistfight, you are probably better off concealing those emotions for the time being.

We have found, however, that incongruity is best used as a signal. Emotions are difficult to disguise and keep from expressing. For instance, if you are feeling amorous toward your friend's wife you run the risk of somehow betraying your feelings. In addition to this risk of inadvertent expression, your ability to fully enjoy and participate in the situation will certainly be diminished by having to constantly monitor how you are expressing yourself. Being with your friends will therefore be much less pleasant and involving than it would otherwise be. For these reasons, it is best to use the need to be incongruent as a signal that what you really need to do is to change to another emotion.

By shifting to another emotion you make it possible for you to be congruent, which makes it possible to be fully responsive to what is going on around you. It is better for the uncertain person leading the child to actually *feel* self-assured than it is to pretend to self-assurance. If the child should detect that the guide is actually only putting up a front of confidence, he may become even more alarmed than if he had been faced with an uncertain guide to begin with. Furthermore, the effort involved in projecting that self-assurance will both blunt the experience for the guide and preoccupy him or her at a time when attention needs to be focused wholly on the possible dangers on the path (the reason for feeling concerned in the first place).

Similarly, the man who is feeling amorous toward his friend's wife will have a much more enjoyable time with the two of them if he is instead feeling affection, friendship, or respect for her. These are all emotions that can be fully expressed without jeopardizing the friendship. The man who is being insulted in the bar will be much safer if he is not sitting there trying to keep the lid on his expression of anger and contemptuousness, but has instead shifted his emotional state to feeling wary or tolerant—emotions that he could more appropriately express in the situation he happens to be in.

When you do recognize that you are being or have been incongruent, that is the time to shift either to a way of accessing a more appropriate emotion (if you already know what you would rather be feeling), or to the During or After selection formats (if you do not already know how you would rather feel). Once you have done that, the flexibility of expression made possible by the format presented in this chapter will help you express yourself in a way that is satisfying and effective.

## *What You Have Now*

You now have a format that will enable you to choose how you express yourself emotionally. Through the use of that format you can generate ways of expression that you have only seen others use or, in fact, can create ways that are entirely new to you. In addition, the format helps ensure that the modes of expression that you do choose for yourself are ones that "fit" who you are, and are appropriate for whatever outcomes you want fulfilled by expressing yourself in the situation. But why should you bother with all that?

The only way anyone has of knowing anything about you is by how you express yourself. It started when you were first born and your parents decided you were a docile baby because you were so quiet, or a happy baby because you smiled a lot, and so on. It continues today when your friends think you are feeling shy because you are so quiet at parties, or that you are feeling superior because you often smile when they tell you their problems. But it may be that you are feeling unconnected, rather than shy, at parties, or that you are feeling nervous, rather than superior, when they tell you their problems. Will Rogers used to twirl his lariat and interpret the life of our country to millions of people, explaining, "All I know is what I read in the papers." The only thing people know about you is what they read in your emotional expressions.

Most people take what is, essentially, a genetic point of view when it comes to emotional expression. They assume that how people express themselves is causally attributable to certain emotions and personal qualities. The same way that they know that George's blue eyes are the expression of two recessive genes for eye color, they "know" that when George smiles at his friend's problems he is expressing his feeling of superiority. And if George himself accepts the "genetics" of emotions, then even if he is aware that he is not expressing himself accurately to others he will believe that there is nothing he can do about it, other than letting his friends know that he is feeling nervous when he smiles, not superior.

Expression is the ultimate communication. It is the interface between you and the world around you. Expression can also be an interface between you and your understanding of yourself. You can probably recall moments when, for whatever reason, you surprised yourself by behaving in a way that was, for you, unusual or utterly new, but was also utterly congruent with how you were feeling. For many of us these moments come when we are alone and feel free to let down the veil of whatever public persona we have been maintaining. Whether those moments of surprising self-expression were pleasant or unpleasant, they were almost certainly revealing, probably putting you in touch with emotions that you had been neglecting or were even wholly unaware of. Even when you are alone, having a choice about expressing your emotions accurately can be fulfilling in and of itself.

Having choice about emotional expression, then, can make it possible for you to better communicate who you are as a person to others and to yourself. What kind of world would it be if everyone had choice about how to express their emotions? It would be a world in which people responded to the actual, rather than assumed, needs and experiences of those around them. Daily, each of us would have the gratifying experience of being *understood* by our families, friends, and workmates. A society in which the actual emotional needs and experiences of its members are clear is a society in which people feel understood rather than misunderstood, connected rather than isolated, and trusting rather than fearful of expression.

10

# *Employing Your Emotions*

THE FLEXIBILITY, CONGRUENCY, AND EFFECTIVENESS MADE possible by the formats in the previous chapters not only make life easier, they make it more satisfying and rewarding as well. But what about those unpleasant emotions that no one is likely to ask for, but that we all nevertheless experience at one time or another? Now that you have some tools for emotional choice, should you use those tools to eliminate all unpleasant emotions from your life?

Loneliness, guilt, fear, overwhelmed, anxiety, jealousy, frustration, regret, anger—most of us try to avoid these emotions, feel terrible about ourselves when we can't, are at our least resourceful when experiencing them, and wish that we could cut them out of our lives entirely. But there is a better choice than such emotional surgery.

In Chapter 3 we introduced the notion that your emotions are like caring friends, letting you know about a situation that needs your attention. They may be telling you something that is unpleasant, and they may be delivering the news in a way that is painful to hear. Nevertheless, it would be as foolish to ignore what your emotional advisor is trying to tell you as it would be to amputate your legs if they began to ache during a long hike, or to cut off your nose if it started to burn after a long day in the sun.

No matter how unpleasant, odious, or awful an emotion seems to you to be, it is actually worth having *as a signal.* As we discussed in Chapter 3, what that emotional signal is trying to tell you is called the *functional attribute* of the emotion. Even the most unpleasant emotions have functional attributes and can be useful if you respond to them as important signals about your needs.

Employing your emotions is the third key ability to emotional choice, and the very heart of emotional employment is the functional attribute. Once the functional attribute is specified for a particular emotion, it immediately transforms that emotion into a feeling worth having and using. For instance, it is worthwhile to feel regret, guilt, or frustration—that is, it is worthwhile to know when you have made a mistake, violated your standards, or are still striving toward an outcome—provided that becoming aware of those things is the impetus to summon an appropriate response.

Too often, however, these emotions are felt and expressed but not responded to. There is little point in regretting something you have done unless that feeling of regret helps you change your future behavior. There is little point in feeling guilty unless your feeling of guilt leads to a renewal of will and intention to fulfill your standards in the future. There is little point in feeling frustrated unless that feeling of frustration propels you toward creative efforts to attain your goal. The functional attribute of an unpleasant emotion *specifies what you need to do to respond appropriately to that emotion.*

As we have demonstrated in different ways throughout this book, emotions such as regret, guilt, apprehension, overwhelmed, jealousy, and anger are all worth having if used well. In fact, as we pointed out earlier, if you could not have these emotions you would be at a great disadvantage. If you never felt regret, you would never become aware that there was something that you could have and should have done differently. Not having gotten that signal, you would miss out on the opportunity to change how you handle that same situation the next time it comes up. Without the signaling feeling of guilt, you would not know that you had violated one of your standards, and so would probably violate that same standard again and again. Moving through life without any moments of apprehension would make it easy for you to step on the toes of others—or into hot water. If you never felt overwhelmed you might squander your time working on low-priority outcomes. The inability to feel jealous could turn you into someone for whom relationships are interchangeable and easily replaceable. And if you never felt angry you could be easily mistaken for a doormat. Obviously, when seen in the light of their signal value, even terribly unpleasant emotions gain a luster that makes them worth having.

These emotions really become worth having, however, when they propel you toward useful outcomes and behaviors.

## *The Generative Chain*

The most effective means we know of for transforming unpleasant emotions into the valued impetus for setting outcomes and initiating useful behaviors is the *generative chain*. The generative chain was the first technique we developed when we started our search for remedies that would free us from the effects of debilitating emotions—especially ones that formed recurring themes in our lives. The generative chain uses the functional attribute of an emotion to set an outcome, and then "chains" that initial emotion to other emotions that lead you to an appropriately resourceful state.

We call it "chaining" because the result is very much like a chain with the links forged of emotions. A sequence of emotions is created that, once initiated by the triggering of the unpleasant emotion, fires off automatically and sequentially. Such sequencing of emotions can be found naturally in all of us—although usually not in the service of useful outcomes.

In a common example of a negative sequence, a person begins

by feeling overwhelmed, which leads him to feeling inadequate, then hopeless, and finally depressed. Through such a chain, within a matter of moments an individual can transport himself from feeling overwhelmed to the paralysis of depression. People can chain themselves from feeling vulnerable to anxious to fearful to paralyzing fear, or from impatience to frustration to anger to rage. One very common chain takes people from feeling jealous to angry, and feeling rejected naturally takes many of us to feeling either unworthy or angry. These chains of one emotion leading to another occur as a direct result of how the person is thinking, as illustrated in the following example.

Sheila is representative of the 80's woman. She represents numerous outcomes to herself—taking care of the children's health, monitoring their progress in school, fulfilling social commitments, exercising, meeting financial goals, fulfilling her work responsibilities, etc., etc. Sheila perceives all of these outcomes as needs rather than as desires. And she sees them all right in front of her, in one large overlapping mass, that *all need to be done right now.* Of course she feels overwhelmed.

The fact that she believes that all of these outcomes need to be done, and that she is not getting them all done *now,* is used by Sheila as evidence that she is inadequate; and accordingly she feels inadequate. After all, if she were adequate then she would have all these things accomplished. She confirms her diagnosis by looking around at other people who (again, to her eyes) do accomplish these kinds of outcomes, and still seem to have time left over for other pursuits.

Of course she realizes that, because she is inadequate, the situation is hopeless. When she looks into the future, she sees no hope of anything being different and so feels hopeless about both the situation and herself.

Through the dingy lens of hopelessness, the world looks gloomy. The past has been miserable and the future will be the same—to Sheila it seems as though she is looking up at the world from the bottom of a well on a dark and cloudy night. From there it's an easy slide into feeling depressed.

What takes Sheila from one emotional link to the next is a set of perceptions and associations—her way of thinking about things. Once such a chain of thoughts, emotions, and behaviors has been forged, it tends to continue to function consistently and compellingly.

Although they are often a source of unpleasantness and resourcelessness, you can also use the consistent and compelling nature of such chains to great advantage and satisfaction, if you are properly oriented. The proper orientation, of course, is toward worthwhile outcomes, rather than toward resourceless, paralyzing ones.

Suppose that instead of using her feeling of being overwhelmed as evidence of her inadequacy, Sheila responds to that feeling as a signal that she is holding constant more outcomes to be accomplished than she can accomplish in the time available. In other words, that feeling of being overwhelmed means that she needs to reevaluate and set priorities on her outcomes.

Because Sheila feels a combination of respect and appreciation for the valuable emotional signal she has received, she slows herself down and takes a look at her outcomes. Looking at her situation with a feeling of curiosity, she realizes that some of the outcomes she has been setting for herself might be nice to fulfill, but they are not really necessary and, given the constraints on her time, could well be dropped for now. Taking the outcomes that remain she sets priorities on them according to how important they are, when they can be done, and so on.

Sheila next recalls times when she has accomplished a great many outcomes in an effective fashion. There was the time that papers were due in every one of her college classes. She got them written, and she did a good job. And there was the time she nursed her child back to health after a serious accident, while at the same time beginning a new job and orchestrating the reconciliation between her husband and his brother. Her memories of being more than adequate to the task help Sheila to feel reassured about her capability. Looking back over these examples of capability, she can see that when her priorities are clear, she can get things done.

By imagining herself in the future actually accomplishing the outcomes she has set for herself, Sheila begins to feel confident of her ability to eventually attain her outcomes.

Sheila has just taken herself through a generative chain. She went from overwhelmed to respectful/appreciative, from respectful/appreciative to curious, from curious to reassured, and from reassured to confident. The sequence may sound somewhat lengthy and complicated, but it's not really more complicated than what you take yourself through in delivering yourself from overwhelmed into depression. How difficult this (or any) chain feels to you depends on how familiar you are with thinking along the lines inherent in that chain. The results, however, make becoming familiar with such empowering chains very much worth the effort.

The generative chain guides your attention along a satisfying and effective path, rather than allowing you to wander off and possibly end up thrashing around in the brambles. Sheila's journey through the generative chain format took her through a chain of emotions that is forged each time the format is used, beginning with the one she found unpleasant and debilitating (this time, overwhelmed), then to respectful/appreciative, then to curious, then to reassured, and finally to confident. Each of the links in this chain is a manifestation of, and reinforced by, the kind of thinking that is needed at each of those emotional steps.

The recognition of the functional attribute makes it possible for you to reorient yourself toward a useful outcome and response to the unpleasant emotion that you are feeling. Knowing that feeling vulnerable is a signal that you need to do something to take care of yourself immediately sets as your outcome: *Do something to take care of yourself.* Any emotion that alerts you to the fact that you need to do something to take care of yourself (such as vulnerable), that you need to find another option (such as stuck), or that you need to reevaluate and set priorities on your outcomes (such as overwhelmed), etc., is an emotion worth respecting and appreciating.

It may strike you as odd to feel respectful and appreciative toward feelings of vulnerability, or being stuck, or overwhelmed. Remember, however, that people who do exceptionally well at recovering from illness are those who respond to their symptoms as signals (information, feedback) about what is going on with them, and therefore what they need to respond to. Certainly they don't enjoy their symptoms, but they are grateful for, and attentive to, the signals that make it possible for them to respond appropriately, rather than hating those symptoms for the discomfort they bring. Similarly, unpleasant emotions are experiential "symptoms" of what is amiss in how you are currently doing things.

Taking its theme from the functional attribute of the emotion, the generative chain leads you through a sequence in which you become curious about what you need to do in relation to the functional attribute; recall reassuring experiences of having done in other contexts what you need to do now; and imagine yourself in the future, doing what you need to do.

The chain is designed to make available to you the best use of the debilitating emotion that you have been feeling, as well as give you access to what your own personal history has to offer in terms of resources and understandings. The generative chain takes you through responding to your present needs and accessing your past resources, and then propels you into a more fulfilled future.

Here are the generative chains for ten emotions that can be particularly pernicious. Read through all of them, or skip to the ones that are of most interest to you. The examples that follow show how the generative chain works and how it is used; you can use these sequences to take you from being paralyzed to being confident and purposeful. For your convenience, we have included each of the generative chain formats, with each step separately numbered, in "The Formats at a Glance" section at the end of the book. But remember, to forge a generative chain you have to do more than read about it, you need to take yourself through the format. Each time you do, you will be strengthening the chain and helping ensure that it will pull you in a useful direction whenever your emotions let you know you could use the help.

## *Regret*

John, a young trainee of ours, repeatedly took his anger and frustrations from work out on his fiancée at home. Each time he used her as an emotional punching bag, he immediately regretted his behavior. It upset her, ruined their evening together, and put an unnecessary strain on their relationship. Nevertheless, hardly a week would pass before he would have a hard day at the office and would again find himself staring into her tear-filled eyes as he castigated her for some minor failure.

Upon learning the generative chain for regret, John sat down and carefully took himself through it. He began by recalling his feeling of regret about the last time he had come home and fumed at his fiancée. Respecting the valuable emotional signal he had received, he recognized that *his feeling of regret was letting him know that he needed to do something to ensure that he did not repeat such a detrimental tirade in the future.* With a feeling of curiosity, John then considered what he could have done differently that would have been more in accord with the kind of interaction he wanted to have with his fiancée. Realizing that he was misplacing his anger by attacking his fiancée, John decided that they would have a much better interaction if he told her that he was feeling angry about things that had happened at work, and that he would like to talk about it. With this approach they would both feel that they were doing something for their relationship, and he would be able to be much calmer and listen to her feedback and questions, rather than simply complaining at her.

Satisfied with his plan, John recalled times when he had shared his feelings with other people, and times when he had asked others for their attention and help. As he reviewed those occasions, he felt reassured about his ability to do what he needed to do. Finally, he imagined the next time he came home from the office feeling angry and enraged. He imagined coming home, ready to burst, taking his fiancée by the hand, telling her how he was feeling, and asking her if she would talk about it with him. He ran through this scenario until he felt confident of his ability to do what he needed to do.

In using the generative chain, John took himself through a sequence of emotions that began with feeling regret, then progressed to respect/appreciation, to curious, to reassured, and finally to confident. Once he was familiar with the chain, it took him quickly and easily from feeling regretful to feeling confident about his ability to share his feelings and ask for attention.

The first step in the generative chain for regret is to recognize that you are feeling regretful. Next, feel respectful and appreciative toward your feeling of regret as being a signal that you need to do something to ensure that you don't repeat the same mistake in the future.

With a feeling of curiosity, evaluate your mistake with respect to what you could have done to avoid making it. Recall memories of mistakes you have made (past sources of regrets) that you corrected once you knew what to do. Use these examples as a basis for feeling reassured.

Finally, imagine a future situation in which you do what you have identified should have been done in the situation you feel regretful about. Make this rich and vivid rehearsal of the future compelling enough that it fills you with confidence about your ability to actually fulfill that future.*

This chain takes you through a correction and resolution of what you have been regretting, leaving you feeling confident about the future and free to turn your attention elsewhere. This is far better than sitting around castigating yourself for some mistake or wrong you have committed. If you are a person who frequently experiences regret that leaves you feeling just awful and with nowhere useful to go, then it will be worth your while to make this generative chain for regret one of your automatic responses.

### *Frustration*

Frustration is what you might feel when you have just been informed that your grade in calculus was an improvement but not quite good enough to pass, and so you are going to have to take the class for the third time; or when you have been unsuccessfully trying to get it through your son's seemingly impenetrable skull that drinking and driving do not mix; or when you have just finished your fourth crash diet this year and your new bathing suit still doesn't fit. Few people enjoy feeling frustrated. But whether you enjoy it or not, feeling frustrated means that you are still engaged in attaining some goal or outcome that you have set for yourself. The significance of feeling frustrated—that is, its functional attribute—is that *it is a signal to you that you need to change how you are going about trying to attain your outcome.* If you are at the point of frustration, then obviously the approach that you have been taking so far has not been successful.

The generative chain for frustration begins when you recognize that you are feeling frustrated in a particular situation. Feel respectful and appreciative toward your feeling of frustration as being a signal that you need to do something different in terms of learning, changing your perspective, readjusting your expectations, or varying your behavior.

With a feeling of curiosity, evaluate whether the outcome is still worth going after. If it's not, then drop the outcome and go

*If you want more instruction in how to make an imagined future real enough to affect your feelings, read the "Compelling Futures" section in Chapter 3 of *Know How: Guided Programs for Inventing Your Own Best Future*, by Cameron-Bandler, Gordon, and Lebeau.

on to other pursuits. If it is, then continue on with the next step.

Search through your past for experiences in which you overcame similar difficulties by changing your approach. Feel reassured by the fact that you have successfully overcome obstacles.

As a final step, imagine yourself in the future, responding to situations that you find frustrating by changing your approach, and then attaining your outcome, feeling confident about your ability to do that.

For example, suppose that after enduring yet another crash diet, you have just tried on your new swim suit and it still doesn't fit. And let's say that you feel frustrated about this, rather than disappointed, angry, or hopeless. Once you recognize that you are feeling frustrated about getting your body to look the way you want it to, the next step is to realize that your feeling of frustration is a signal that you need to change how you are going about trying to lose weight. In addition, you need to respect your emotion as an important signal that is helping you to prevent repeating what has already proved unsuccessful.

The next thing you need to do is to consider, with feelings of curiosity, whether losing weight and fitting into that bathing suit is an outcome that is still worth going after. If you decide that it is not, then, perhaps with a sigh of relief, you can let go of the goal of getting into that swim suit. If it continues to be a worthwhile outcome, then you need to find examples from your past of times when you have changed your approach to achieving some goal and thereby succeeded in attaining that goal. Finding enough such examples will reorient you toward more flexibility in your thinking as well as reassure you that you have the ability to change your approach to achieving your goal—in this case, losing weight. Finally you step into the future, imagining yourself responding with new approaches to attaining outcomes that frustrate you, and feeling confident about your ability to do so.

Once you have gone through this chain, you will not be feeling frustrated. And more important, you will be reoriented toward, and feeling confident about, discovering another, perhaps more effective way of attaining the outcome you have set for yourself.

### *Anxiety*

Anxiety is something you might feel on your way to an IRS audit, while making an appointment to see your doctor to have a lump checked, or when you are about to meet your prospective in-laws for the first time. The anxiety you feel at such times is usually the result of either imagining an unpleasant future, or of making images of a future that is either unclear or unknown, and therefore a wide-open source of negative possibilities. The functional attribute of anxiety is as *a signal to you that you need to prepare to cope with or to avoid possible negative consequences of an upcoming situation.*

As with all generative chains, the first step in the chain for anxiety is to recognize that you are feeling anxious. Then remember that feeling anxious is a signal to you that there is something in your future for which you need to better prepare, and feel respect and appreciation for that emotion as a vital signal.

With a feeling of curiosity, evaluate what you need to do to better prepare. This may involve gathering information to fill in your picture of the future, marshalling or acquiring certain skills, or establishing a positively stated outcome.

Recall examples from your past when you have done what you now need to do to meet this future challenge or threat, feeling reassured as you recall these memories of your capability.

Finally, imagine yourself in the future preparing to meet the challenge or threat, repeating this rehearsal until you feel confident about your ability to do what you need to do.

The preparation you need to do depends upon what it is you are facing in the future that you are feeling anxious about now. For instance, if you are feeling anxious about how a certain person will respond to your dinner invitation, your preparation may be a matter of gathering information. This information may come from others (interacting with your prospective date more to get a better idea about how he or she will respond; asking others who know him or her what they think the response will be), or it may come from you (searching your own experiences with this person for indications of how he or she responds to you and to such invitations).

Adequate preparation may also mean accessing or acquiring certain skills that you need in order to meet what you are facing in a satisfactory way. For example, suppose that you are feeling anxious about how best to present your material in a speech you have agreed to deliver. If organizing material for presentation is something that you already know how to do, you can access that skill and go to work. If it is not a skill that you already have, you may need to go to someone who can teach you how to do it. Similarly, adequate preparation for your speech may involve learning how to speak in a way that others will find interesting, or perhaps how to field questions.

Finally, adequate preparation may mean changing a negatively stated outcome to one that is positively stated. The source of your anxiety may be a negatively stated outcome such as, "I don't want to blow it," "I'll look like a fool if I try it," or "I won't be able to handle things if it turns out that way." Each of these outcomes says what you do *not* want to have happen, and each tells you only what *not* to do. Outcomes that are stated in the positive, however, provide you with a direction. Knowing where you do want to go is much more reassuring than knowing where you don't want to go. In addition, once you know where you want to go, you will have a better idea of what to do in order to get there.

As with all of the emotions described in this chapter, the value in feeling anxious is in the feedback it provides you. When that feedback goes unrecognized, anxiety becomes an unpleasant, even paralyzing experience. The outcome of this chain, however, is to take you from being paralyzed to feeling confident about your ability to do what you need to do to prepare yourself for what you believe is coming. Such a positive emotional state frees your experiential and behavioral resources, motivating you to act, rather than to wait and tremble.

### *Hopelessness*

Your soufflé has come out looking like a pancake for the tenth time, and you drop into the feeling of hopelessness—you will *never* be able to make a decent soufflé. You might also feel hopeless about your spouse's drinking, about your child's choice of a mate, or about the possibility of your friend's troubled marriage staying together. What your feeling of hopelessness is trying to tell you, its functional attribute, is that *it is time to let go.* If you have done all that you can and it wasn't enough, it's time to move on to other outcomes.

You start the generative chain for hopelessness by recognizing that you are feeling hopeless. Next, feel respectful and appreciative toward your feeling of hopelessness as a signal that it's time to let go of some outcome that you have been unsuccessfully striving to attain.

With a feeling of curiosity, evaluate whether there is anything else that you can reasonably do. If your answer is yes, then go to feeling frustrated as a first step to feeling challenged and determined, and to generating alternative ways to try to get what you want. If the answer is no, go on to the next step.

Recall examples from your past of times when you let go of certain outcomes, large or small, and thereby freed yourself to turn to other things. Find enough examples so that you feel reassured about your ability to do this.

And finally, imagine yourself in the future, walking away from this outcome that simply can't be attained, feeling confident about your ability to do that and to turn your efforts toward outcomes that *can* be accomplished.

People often feel hopeless about something when they have in fact not yet exhausted their possibilities of doing something to attain their outcomes. Accordingly, the third step in this generative chain is very important when you are responding to your feelings of hopelessness, for in that step you consider whether there is anything else that might be worth your while to try. For instance, suppose that your spouse is an alcoholic. Perhaps you have tried encouraging suggestions, threatening, pleading, and ignoring, all to no avail, and now you feel hopeless about ever changing him or her. Your feeling of hopelessness is telling you that it is time to let go of your desire to change your spouse. But *is* it time?

To answer this question, consider what else you could do that would be worthwhile (step 3 in the chain). If you can think of nothing else to do—other than, say, offering your spouse money to quit, which you reject as not being a worthwhile approach—then it is time to heed your feelings of hopelessness and let go of the outcome of changing your mate. If, however, you can think of something worthwhile yet to be tried, such as contacting AA, an alcoholic treatment program, or counselor, then it is not appropriate to feel hopeless. Instead, step into feeling challenged or determined, so that you can mobilize your behavioral resources to attain your outcome using the new approach you have decided upon.

### *Stuck*

All of us have had the experience of wanting to move forward with something while at the same time being at a loss as to how to proceed. When you can't find words to express an idea you are trying to convey, or you don't know how to get a piece of heavy furniture up the stairs, or you realize that your career is at a seemingly permanent standstill, the paralysis of feeling stuck may steal over you, robbing you of both the will and the means to move forward. Feeling stuck, then, is *a signal that you need to find another option, stepping away from the approaches you have been taking and finding other ways to attain your goals.*

The generative chain for feeling stuck begins when you realize that you feel stuck. Recognize that you need to generate other options for yourself in this situation, and feel respectful and appreciative toward the important emotional signal you have given yourself.

With a feeling of curiosity, evaluate the approaches to which you have been confining yourself in trying to attain your outcome.

Recall times when you have been stuck and have changed how you were thinking about the situation so that you were able to generate another way to go; feel reassured about your ability to do this.

Go into the future, imagining yourself feeling stuck and then generating new options that make it possible for you to keep moving forward. Repeat and make these futures increasingly vivid until you feel confident about your ability to generate new options when you feel stuck.

This chain orients you toward stepping outside of the boundaries within which you are currently operating. The chain provides you with an opportunity to come up with new options for proceeding toward your outcome. These options may include getting advice or help from others.

### *Anger*

We all have our own criteria, our own standards, regarding how people should behave, and when we perceive that those criteria have been violated, we often feel angry. For instance, you might feel angry when you see a child being mistreated, or when another car cuts ahead of you in traffic, or when your mate disregards a serious concern of yours. The functional attribute of feeling angry is as *a signal that an important criterion of yours has been violated.*

The generative chain for anger begins when you recognize

that you are feeling angry. Let that be the reminder to feel respectful and appreciative toward your feeling of anger as an important signal letting you know that someone, possibly yourself, has violated an important standard of yours.

With a feeling of curiosity, evaluate what you can do in the future to prevent your standard from being similarly violated, and how you could more usefully respond when your standard is violated despite your efforts to prevent it. If you don't know what to do, gather information from people who seem to be able to respond usefully to such angering situations.

Recall past times when you have prevented or usefully responded to the violation of your standards, and feel reassured about your ability to do it.

Imagine the next time your standard might be violated and see yourself doing something to prevent it from happening. Rerun this future until you feel confident about your ability to respond in the way that you would like to.

It may be that, despite your best efforts, you can't prevent others from violating your standards. Therefore, you should also imagine your standards being violated anyway and how you could respond more usefully. (You may need to turn to the formats in the contextualizing and accessing chapters to help you with this step.) Again, rerun this future until you feel confident that you will be able to respond in a satisfying and effective way.

For instance, suppose that you are driving on the freeway when another car rudely and dangerously cuts you off. As you always do on such occasions, you become furious at that anonymous driver. Not wanting to react in that way in the future to such situations, you take yourself through the generative chain for anger. Once you have recognized your anger as an important signal about the violation of a standard that you value, you then consider what you can do in the future to respond usefully to being cut off in traffic, or to prevent it from happening again. In terms of prevention, you might find that you could be more vigilant about drivers coming up from behind you. But being vigilant won't always prevent someone from cutting in ahead of you. So you also need a better way to respond when it does happen. For instance, you could feel relieved that you are safe, and feel sorry for that other driver who takes so little care with his own life. You then find memories of narrow escapes that left you feeling relieved, and memories of feeling sorry for others when you could see them heading down a personally destructive road. Reassured that you can respond in these ways, you step into the future, imagining incidents in which careless drivers endanger you, and in which you respond by feeling relieved and sorry for the transgressors, and perhaps concern for the innocent drivers up ahead that are still in danger.

We recognize that starting with feeling angry and then moving through this chain is not always easy to do, but it is well worth the effort. The evaluation of step 3 in this generative chain helps a great deal in that it provides you with a disengaged opportunity to decide whether the violation is *worth* being angry about.

## *Guilt*

It sometimes happens that the person who violates your standards is you. If you don't believe in the rod but nevertheless apply it to your child's backside, you are faced with the unpleasant fact of having violated your own standards. Or perhaps you believe in driving respectfully, but carelessly cut someone off in traffic; or you think that it is wrong to lie, and yet you find yourself lying about a previous engagement to get out of a dinner invitation; or you keep forgetting to write to that friend to whom you owe a letter. Any time you violate a standard of yours, you are likely to feel guilty.

But suppose that you did not feel guilty when you violated your own standards? In the answer to that question lies the significance and functional attribute of guilt. If you had no way of being alerted to the fact that you are violating, or have just violated, your own standards, you would lack the feedback you need to be sure that your deeds match your beliefs. The functional attribute of guilt, then, is as *a signal that you have somehow violated your standards, and that you need to do something to ensure that you don't violate them again in the future.*

The first step of the generative chain for guilt is to recognize that you are feeling guilt in a particular situation. With respect and appreciation, recognize that your feeling guilty is a signal that you have violated a personal standard and that you need to make sure that you do not do it again in the future.

With a feeling of curiosity, evaluate whether the standard you have violated is one that is worth maintaining. If it is not worth maintaining, then you can update, replace, or discard it.

Recall personal experiences in which you lived up to your personal standards, even though it was difficult to do. As you accumulate these examples, feel reassured about your ability to live up to your personal standards.

Finally, imagine living up to your standards in upcoming situations that will severely test you, and feel confident about your ability to do so.

It sometimes happens that the standards for which we hold ourselves accountable, and about which we feel guilty when we violate them, are standards that are no longer worth keeping. For instance, a woman who was raised to believe that the woman's place is in the home may feel guilty about her desire to get out of that home and into a career. Now in her early forties, she may look upon that belief as no longer appropriate, given the world as it is now and who she is as a person. In fact, she may find that she never really embraced this belief as worthwhile, but has merely tried to fulfill it in her external behavior for many years.

If you determine that the standard *is* worth keeping, then it is appropriate to feel guilty about having violated it. It is also appropriate to use that unpleasant feeling to ignite your efforts to ensure that in the future you match your standard. If, however, you determine that your standard is not worth keeping as it is, then you need to either update it, replace it, or discard it. Remember that when you update or replace a standard you have created a new standard that requires fulfillment, just as its predecessor did. It is therefore appropriate and helpful to continue on through steps 4 and 5 for your new standard.

## *Disappointment*

You have opened the last of your birthday gifts and you failed to get the one present you really wanted. How do you feel? Probably disappointed. You might also feel disappointed when the movie you were looking forward to turned out to be lousy, or when your two young children hatch the chicken pox the day before your long-anticipated romantic weekend with your spouse. The disappointment you feel when these things happen should be taken as *a signal that you need to reevaluate your outcomes, perhaps changing them to ones that are more likely to be attainable under the circumstances.*

The generative chain for disappointment starts with the recognition that you feel disappointed. With respect and appreciation, recognize that your feeling of disappointment is a signal that you need to reevaluate your outcomes.

With a feeling of curiosity, evaluate whether what you wanted and did not get is worth continuing to want. If it is, then go to the next step. If what you wanted and did not get is no longer worth wanting, consider what would be more worthwhile to want under the circumstances, then go to the step after the next.

If what you wanted is still worth pursuing, recall memories of persevering and eventually finding ways to get what you wanted, and feel reassured about your ability to do that.

If it is time to find other things to pursue, recall times when you changed goals and eventually succeeded at getting what you wanted, and feel reassured about your ability to do that.

Last, imagine doing what you need to do to eventually get what you now want, adding detail and vividness until you feel confident about that future.

As the functional attribute in this chain indicates, disappointment is a time for reevaluation. We often don't get what we want or expect. If you continue to want "it," then that desired outcome will continue to influence your experience. If the person you are in love with and want to marry turns down your first proposal, perhaps it is worth continuing to want that person to say "yes," and to continue pursuing the relationship. On the other hand, it's not worth holding on to the outcome of wanting a movie to be good that in fact has already turned out to be lousy. Instead, it may be better to exchange that outcome for figuring out what went wrong with the movie technically, or wanting an enjoyable remainder of the evening.

## *Loneliness*

Audrey felt lonely. She had just spent an hour trying to ignore her loneliness, but now it was undeniable. Once she admitted that she was feeling lonely she sneered at herself, "Thirty-five years old and you can't be alone without falling apart? You're so weak, Audrey!" But still she was lonely. She snapped on the TV for company, but every flick of the dial showed her people being together. She pulled the plug on them, then turned to the refrigerator to try to fill the emptiness she felt. A moment later she was on the couch, spooning ice cream from the container while she flipped through a magazine. But there was no escape in food, either. Audrey switched off the light and walked to the window. She stood there in the dark, gazing out at the apartments and houses across the street, at the families silhouetted in the warm glow of the windows. On the sidewalk, couples strolled and friends loitered. "Oh, hell," she muttered out loud, "I'm not staying *here!*" And she went out to a bar, hoping to meet someone.

Feeling lonely is *a signal that we need a particular kind of contact with other people*. Consequently, we often end up confusing "connection" with "affection" and "passion." For example, Audrey recognized her loneliness as a signal she needed contact with others, but she did not recognize what particular *kind* of contact she needed. The generative chain for loneliness includes an important step in which you evaluate just what kind of contact you want, and with whom, so that your efforts can be mobilized toward truly appropriate and satisfying contacts.

The generative chain for loneliness starts when you recognize that you are feeling lonely. With respect and appreciation, recognize your feeling as a signal of your need for a particular kind of contact or connection with someone.

With a feeling of curiosity, evaluate what kind of contact you want and with whom.

Search through your memories to find examples of times when you initiated such contact, and feel reassured about your ability to make contact with others.

Step into the future and imagine yourself initiating the kind of contact you want to have with the people you have chosen, increasing the vividness of your pictures until you feel confident about your future ability.

When using this chain, be sure that you recall those experiences in which *you* initiated the contact. For instance, the time a dear friend called you up and asked to spend the evening with you may be a lovely memory, and perhaps reassures you that you are wanted, but it will not help you respond appropriately to feeling lonely because it will tend to keep you waiting for the phone to ring again. It's much more useful to recall the times when *you* did the calling.

### *Jealousy*

You have just met your husband's stunning, witty new secretary. Or an old flame of your wife's takes her out to lunch, and they are gone four hours rather than the promised two. Or you are at a party and your mate has been corralled for the last hour by an attractive and attentive member of the opposite sex. Often such occasions elicit feelings of jealousy. For many people, their emotional well-being is tied to the special and intimate relationships they share with their mates and close friends. Jealousy is a response to discovering, or suspecting, that that special and intimate relationship is threatened, which threatens one's emotional well-being as well. The functional attribute of jealousy, then, is as *a signal that you need to do something to protect your emotional well-being.*

The generative chain for jealousy begins when you recognize that you are feeling jealous. With respect and appreciation for the signal value of feeling jealous, recognize that your jealousy is a signal that you need to take care of your emotional well-being.

With a feeling of curiosity, evaluate whether your well-being actually is in jeopardy. If it's not, then move to enjoying the fact that your loved one is having a good time with others. If it is, proceed with the two last steps.

Recall times in your past when you have taken care of yourself; find enough examples so that you feel reassured about your ability to do what you need to in order to maintain your well-being.

As a last step, look to the future and imagine yourself successfully taking care of yourself in situations in which there really is a threat to your well-being. Be sure that these futures are vivid enough to make you feel confident.

There are three patterns that work to generate jealousy, and two of those three patterns can be remedied by using this generative chain. First, if you have low self-esteem you may very well believe that you can be easily replaced. One of the consequences of thinking you can be easily replaced is that the world seems populated with challengers for your position. Every new person with whom your mate interacts, each new interest your mate develops, is perceived as a threat. In this case, the generative chain can be used to build self-esteem by identifying examples of times when you made your mate feel happier (or more appreciated, loved, or fulfilled) with you than he or she could have been with anyone else, and then by rehearsing how you will do that again in the future until you build a state of confidence.*

A second pattern that generates jealousy is the use of criteria that are too possessive. If you view your mate as someone you "own," each new interesting person is perceived as trying to horn in on "your" territory. If you use these kinds of criteria, you probably spend a lot of time struggling—pulling in the reins in an effort to keep your mate from busting out of the corral. It is easy to feel jealous. Any behavior on your mate's part for which you didn't give prior permission is a challenge to your authority, and therefore a threat to your well-being. In this case, what is needed is not a generative chain, but rather a change of criteria to those that are more appropriate to sustaining mutually enhancing relationships. One of our books, *The EMPRINT Method: A Guide to Reproducing Competence* (with David Gordon), contains methods for evaluating and changing criteria.

The third pattern is to be faced with an actual threat, not just a perceived one. If you are using appropriate criteria in your relationship, have strong self-esteem, and are being the person you most want to be, and your mate is actually considering replacing you, you have good reason to feel jealous. In this case, you need to proceed with care. The generative chain will make it possible for you to give your mate all that you can and want to give, by ensuring you are in emotional states that allow you to be most resourceful. You can also use it to prepare for a confrontation, if necessary. And under the worst circumstance, you can use it to generate behaviors that have the best chance of persuading your mate to work with you to preserve your relationship, perhaps by going to couple therapy or by taking each other through the "Relationship Evaluator" and "Threshhold Neutralizer" presented in Leslie Cameron-Bandler's book *Solutions: Practical and Effective Antidotes for Sexual and Relationship Problems.*

* The link between low self-esteem and jealousy is so prevalent that we have produced a videotape titled "Lasting Feelings" that demonstrates how to use the generative chain to deal with this cause of jealousy. If you are interested in knowing more about this videotape, write us at P.O. Box 1173, San Rafael, CA 94915 and we'll send you more information.

If any of the emotions in the previous sections are ones that you frequently experience, it will be worth your while to become accustomed to thinking yourself through the appropriate generative chain. In fact, even if none of these emotions is one that troubles you, we suggest that you go through the generative chain sequence for each one, using some current or recent example as the content. By doing this you will resolve a specific nagging incident; more important, you will be making yourself more familiar with the essential pattern that underlies all generative chains:

*Triggering emotion*
→ *Respect/appreciation*
→ *Curiosity*
→ *Reassurance*
→ *Confidence*

To make a generative chain your own, operating naturally and automatically, it is necessary to take yourself through it several times, each time using a different incident or situation as the content. For example, if you frequently feel guilty and you would like to incorporate the generative chain for guilt as one of your natural responses, you can take yourself first through the chain using as the content the fact that you didn't take your kids to the zoo last week as you had promised. Having done that, go through the sequence again, this time using as content your guilty feelings about scraping someone's car in a parking lot and driving off without leaving a note. Then go through the sequence a third time, using as the content the time you lost your temper with your parents. The goal is to keep taking yourself through the chain until you discover that you are beginning to automatically leap ahead through the steps.

The generative chain works best not just with the emotions we have used as examples in this chapter, but with any emotion that has something to offer you in terms of a useful functional attribute. By "useful" we mean *responding in a way that orients you toward setting outcomes.* Too often these unpleasant emotions go undetected or are poorly responded to, and so are allowed to chain themselves into a progressively downward spiral of unpleasantness. Life offers us many opportunities to experience such emotions as envy, inadequacy, concern, dissatisfaction, and so on.

The value of the generative chain lies in its ability to make these unpleasant emotions work for you.

## *What You Have Now*

The third key ability of emotional choice is Employment: the skill of putting unpleasant emotions to work in a way that supports your best interests. The information presented in this chapter gives you the means to deliver on the promise of full employment.

You now have a new perspective on unpleasant and unwanted emotions. You know that those emotions are worth having, provided you respond to them in a useful way. This is made possible by recognizing the *functional attribute* of the emotion, which specifies what the emotion is doing for you that is useful.

The next step is to respond in an appropriate way to the functional attribute of the emotion. The *generative chain* does just that by taking you through a way of thinking, and a resulting sequence of emotions, that leads you from the unpleasant emotion to feeling confident about your ability to use your resources to respond more usefully in the future.

We have described in detail the generative chains for regret, frustration, anxiety, hopelessness, stuck, anger, guilt, disappointment, loneliness, and jealousy. But these are not merely examples of the chain—they can be used by you or with someone else to change forever your response to those unpleasant emotions.

# 11

# *Prevention*

AFTER SPENDING A WHOLE CHAPTER TELLING YOU THAT even unpleasant emotions have functional attributes that make them worth feeling, we are now ready to admit that there may also be emotions that you simply do not want to reexperience. Functional attribute or no functional attribute, you may want never again to endure feeling humiliated, or lonely, or despairing, or helpless, fearful, hateful, rejected, or unworthy. Perhaps it's just not worth it to you to reexperience one of these very unpleasant emotions. Well, there is a way you can do just that.

When we speak of preventing the recurrence of unpleasant emotions we don't mean that you will *never* feel these emotions again. If it were possible for you to never feel humiliated or fearful or despairing again, the price you would pay would be exacted from your humanity. Such emotions are part of being alive and human. You can, however, usefully and appropriately prevent them from recurring in *certain situations.*

Andrea felt humiliated. At the party last night, her boyfriend, Sam, had gotten drunk and berated her in front of their friends. Facing Sam's boorish behavior, while their friends shook their heads and muttered "Poor Andrea," some people would have felt furious, others helpless, and still others vengeful. But for Andrea the situation generated a profound and intolerable feeling of humiliation.

"Intolerable" was the operative word here, for Andrea came to us for help determined that she would not feel that way again. We soon discovered that she usually takes responsibility for her own experience, rejecting the notion that life is something that just happens *to* her. Rather, she believes that she plays a significant role in generating her life experiences. Feeling humiliated was one of those life experiences that she thought she could avoid in the future if she just knew how. We agreed with her, and gave her the "how" that we had developed for our own use to prevent unacceptable emotional experiences.

First, we asked Andrea to review the events of yesterday and last night. She tried to identify for herself what had led up to Sam's behavior by replaying in her mind the events as they transpired. To help her figure out what had gone on, we suggested she view this "movie" of herself in the situation from several points of view, including her own, Sam's, and that of her friends.

As a result of this review she realized that she had insisted that Sam attend the party even though he was exhausted and a bit down from overwork, she knew that he ordinarily couldn't drink in that exhausted state without getting drunk (as opposed to getting pleasantly high), she had pressed the first drink on him when he seemed reluctant to accept one, she had gotten quite drunk herself, and she had then proceeded to generally ignore him, conversed playfully with others, and, from Sam's perspective, probably appeared to be flirting. It was a bitter pill to swallow, but Andrea could now see how she had contributed significantly to her own humiliation. Andrea does not put up with being badly treated by others, and here she realized that she had treated Sam badly and (through him) herself as well. She was adamant that this would not happen again.

Then we turned Andrea to considering what she could have done differently. She arrived at three tentative conclusions: "I could have respected what was going on with Sam and either gone alone to the party or not gone at all. I could have not pressed him to accept drinks. And I could have interacted with him more, as well as including him more in my interactions with others."

Andrea then followed our lead and considered whether in the future she would rather respond in these three ways. Her answer was a resounding Yes! Sam's behavior that night at the party was quite unusual for him and he was feeling very guilty about how he had acted—as was Andrea, now that she recognized her contribution to their mistreatment of each other that evening.

Knowing that wanting to do something and being capable of doing it are two different things, we next had Andrea ask herself if she was sure that she could respond the way she wants. There was nothing in any of those behaviors that was new or even difficult for her. She could remember dozens of times when she had recognized and respected Sam's mood, had specifically included him in interactions, and so on. Yes, she could do those things in similar situations in the future.

But *would* she? That was the final question Andrea had to consider. Without the resolve to actually do what she wanted to do, the behaviors that she knew were within her grasp would remain unexpressed. But it was unacceptable to Andrea to ever again suffer the humiliation she had suffered at the party, and again came the resounding Yes! from deep inside. She started imagining future situations in which Sam's mood was incompatible with social events they had planned, and saw herself noticing his mood and responding to it in a way that fulfilled the behavioral outcomes she set for herself.

Andrea's response to her situation with Sam was the result of her having gone through the *Prevention* format described later in this chapter. This format was distilled from the behavior of people who consistently take responsibility for their own experiences, recognize their mistakes, and then correct them to avoid having to repeat them again in the future. We have found again and again that individuals who go through this sequence may, like anyone else, experience life's most unpleasant emotions, but they usually do so only once or twice before reorganizing their behavior so that they never have to experience them again under those same circumstances.

Perhaps the most appropriate way to characterize these unwanted emotions is to consider them "mistakes," which can be corrected by changing your behavior and/or circumstances. The particular correction that you make will depend upon the results of your evaluation of how you and others contributed to your falling into the unwanted emotion. In Andrea's case, for example, she determined that her humiliation was the result of her failure to pay attention to Sam's moods and needs, pushing him to drink, and ignoring him. The corrections she therefore needed to make in her behavior included learning to recognize and respect Sam's moods and needs, refraining from encouraging him to drink, and making an effort to include him in her interactions at social gatherings.

Suppose that, upon evaluating what had precipitated her humiliating experience, Andrea had discovered that Sam humiliated *everyone*, not just her, when he was tired and drinking. This would be a different situation, leading her to different corrections to avoid the mistake of being humiliated by him again. In this case, Andrea might decide that in the future she would simply take care not to be around Sam when he was drinking.

Or suppose that the result of Andrea's evaluation was the realization that Sam humiliated anyone—including her—whenever the opportunity arose. From this information Andrea would be likely to conclude that ensuring that Sam will never again humiliate her will require that she not be around him at all. In this case, the mistake that needs correcting, if she is to avoid being humiliated, is her being with Sam.

There are times when the awful emotion you have experienced was not a consequence of your behavior. Simply by being in a certain situation you may be accepting an invitation to unpleasantness, as Andrea would be if she were to stay with a man who humiliated people whenever he had the opportunity. Like the Catholic sin of presenting yourself to the occasion of sin, this is the sin of foolishly presenting yourself to the occasion of abuse.

Notice that in none of the possible choices we described for Andrea did we include "change Sam." It is best to proceed as though you have relatively little control when it comes to changing other people. If your desired outcome is to make sure that you never again have to endure a particular emotional response, and the success of that outcome depends upon other people behaving a certain way which for them is unusual or out of character, you are almost certain to fail in attaining your outcome. Andrea, for instance, changed *her* responses, rather than trying to change Sam. It is true that Sam did change as a result of Andrea's change, but his changing was not necessary for Andrea to get her outcome. Unless other people have the awareness and desire to change in just the way that you want them to, it is unlikely that they will do just what you want them to do when you want them to do it. Therefore it is best if the changes that you make are changes in yourself.

With these considerations in mind, here is the format you can use to prevent the recurrence of unwanted emotions.

1. Identify the emotion you are feeling, making sure that it is one that you are unwilling to experience again in the situation in which you felt it.

2. By running a movie in your head of the events leading up to and during the time you felt that emotion, identify what, if anything, you did to contribute to its occurrence. Look at your behavior from at least two points of views—your own and someone else's.

3. Rerunning that internal movie of what happened, identify what, if any, external causes (circumstances, other people's behavior, etc.) contributed to your experiencing the unwanted emotion.

4. Combining your findings from the previous two steps, come up with replacement behaviors (corrections) that would make it impossible for you to experience that unwanted emotion again in that situation.

5. Make sure that you *can* do those replacement behaviors by searching your personal history for examples of your having done them, even if in other types of situations. You may also be able to assure yourself that you can do the replacement behaviors by recalling having seen others do them—examples that you know you could do as well. If you can't find either personal or vicarious examples of the replacement behaviors you will need, then go back to step

4 and come up with other simpler or more familiar behaviors. (If the behaviors you need are not within your present experience and are irreplaceble for getting the outcome you want, then you will need to learn them before you will be able to avoid a recurrence of the emotion-triggering situation.) As a check for yourself, consider the question, How do you know you *can* do the replacement behaviors you will need?

6. Now, *will* you do those replacement behaviors? Is your commitment strong enough? Create a movie in which you see yourself successfully doing the needed behaviors.

   Next, rerun that movie, this time from the perspective of being *within* it, seeing what you would see through your own eyes if you were actually there, hearing what you would hear, and feeling what you would feel. Make sure that your movie is vivid and rich in detail. As a check for yourself, consider the question, How do you know you *will* do these behaviors? (Remember that you are not figuring out what to do once you are in, and want to get out of, that unwanted emotion, but what to do to prevent your getting into that emotion in the first place.)

The following examples use the prevention format for several unpleasant emotions. These are not intended only as examples of how the format works; you should also use them to learn the format by actually taking yourself through the steps for each of the emotions presented.

## *Disappointment*

For our client Jill there were disappointments, and then there were DISAPPOINTMENTS. Jill became aware of the latter category when she was sitting alone at her kitchen table the morning after her birthday and no one—not even her sister, with whom she is very close—had called to wish her a happy one. When she realized that even her sister had forgotten, the disappointment that Jill felt was devastating. A couple of months later, Jill's husband forgot their anniversary, and again Jill felt that devastating disappointment. It was so unpleasant, in fact, that she decided to never have occasion to experience it again.

Taking herself through the Prevention format, Jill realized that she did not foster these occasions for disappointment, and neither did her loved ones' forgetfulness mean that they were uncaring people or that they did not love her. She realized that some people are simply not given to remembering dates or keeping a watchful eye on the calendar, and if it was vital to her that they know about certain dates, then it was up to her to remind them. Accordingly, Jill resolved to begin sending direct but charming reminders about her upcoming birthdays, anniversaries, and other important occasions to everyone who needed to take notice of those dates, or to orchestrate her own celebrations. Jill trusted these important people to care about her, so she informed them directly of her needs.

When have you felt intensely disappointed? Recall a time when you felt very disappointed—so disappointed that you never want to experience that emotion again in such a situation.

Go back over the events leading up to and during your disappointment and consider what, if anything, you did or did not do that contributed to your feeling disappointment. For instance, did you fail to pursue what you wanted to your fullest ability? (You really needed an "A" on the biology exam, but went to the movies instead of studying.) Did you sabotage your own possible good fortune in some way? (You annoyed an important client by failing to return a phone call.) Did you use poor judgment in selecting what you wanted in the first place, in planning how to get it, or in deciding who you could depend upon? (You planned a romantic evening at home as a surprise to your girlfriend, even though she often has last-minute business dinners; or you scheduled a picnic for the first weekend in March, with no contingency plans in case of stormy weather.)

Reviewing the events once again, were there any circumstances that contributed to your feeling disappointed? Did the behavior or circumstances of other people contribute to your disappointment?

Now, using what you have learned about the dynamics involved in creating the occasion for your disappointment, generate a list of replacement behaviors that will keep that disappointment from happening again. Any factors that are based upon circumstances or other people's behavior will require that you remove them from their influential position, or provide an alternative. For instance, if the cause of your disappointment is a friend who often borrows books but fails to return them, you may have to resort to replacement behaviors such as refusing to lend books to him until he returns the ones he's already borrowed.

Make sure that you can do those replacement behaviors. How do you know that you can? For example, perhaps you have done it before, you have seen others do it, or you can imagine yourself doing it and it seems easy.

Consider whether or not you *will* do the replacement behaviors. Run a movie of the future in which you see yourself in a potentially disappointing situation, similar to the one that initiated this whole process, responding this time with the replacement behaviors. Rerun the movie, this time stepping into it so that you see, hear, and feel what you will when you next find yourself in such a situation. Make adjustments in your behavior, and rerun the movie as many times as necessary, until you know that you will do the replacement behaviors.

## *Shame*

Bobbi, a close friend of ours, was enjoying a late night gab session with some girlfriends when she blabbed the details of another friend's marital difficulties—details that had been passed on to her in confidence. This was not the first time she had betrayed a confidence. When she realized that she had done it again, waves of shame washed over her. In the past when she had betrayed such confidences she felt ashamed, but the combined effect of all those times finally created an undertow so strong that she was sucked down as deep as her feelings could go. By the time she finally resurfaced, Bobbi had decided that she would never go through that again.

As Bobbi took herself through the evaluations in the format, she discovered that there was nothing malicious in her gossiping. Instead, it was a matter of her seeming inability to remember the privileged nature of some information, combined with the enthusiasm and joy she experienced when sharing information and stories with others.

How about you? Recall a time when you felt ashamed—so ashamed that you never want to experience that emotion again in such a situation. What, if anything, did you do or not do that contributed to your feeling shame? For instance, did you use poor judgment in getting into the situation in the first place? Were you out of your element? (After two weeks of dance instruction at Arthur Murray's you went to audition as a dancer for a local production of a Broadway musical.) Did you ignore or fail to recognize warnings from yourself or others that you were erring? (You ignored your own body as well as the warnings of your friends when they told you that you'd had enough to drink.) Did you project what was going on in other people's minds, perhaps that they were thinking damning things about you? (You imagined that the other people at your aerobics class think you are fat and weak.)

Reviewing the events once again, were there any outside circumstances or actions by others that contributed to your feeling ashamed?

After Bobbi thought about it for a few moments, the initial replacement behavior that she settled on was to simply ask her friends not to tell her anything that they would not want to be generally known. This worked well immediately, of course, and Bobbi used this "breather" to practice withholding various pieces of information that she heard until she developed the ability to keep confidences.

Generate your own list of replacement behaviors that will keep your shame from happening again—for instance, drinking in moderation instead of becoming shamefully drunk; or voicing your concern in an even-handed manner instead of in a shameful display of screaming and ranting. Make sure that you can do those replacement behaviors. How do you know that you can?

Consider whether you *will* do the replacement behaviors. Run a movie of the future in which you see yourself in a potentially shaming situation, similar to the one that initiated this whole process, responding this time with the replacement behaviors. Rerun the movie, this time stepping inside of it so that you see, hear, and feel what you will when you next find yourself in such a situation. Adjust and repeat this movie as many times as necessary until you are confident that you will do the replacement behaviors.

### *Anger*

When the wax from the half-spent candles finally spilled onto the tablecloth, Jane angrily snuffed out the two flames and flicked on the overhead light. She had worked hard preparing a wonderful dinner and romantic evening, and now Steve was late again. When Steve finally did get home, he was nearly blown back out the door by the fury of Jane's attack on him. When the dust had finally settled, Jane was still vibrating. In fact, both were now vibrating, and for several days their interactions were unpleasant. When at last Jane looked back on that awful evening and the dismal days that followed, she resolved that she would never again go through feeling that furious anger. She decided to seek our help.

When Jane began evaluating what factors had contributed to her anger, one of the first things that struck her was that she had cooked a special meal and made plans for the evening that hinged upon Steve being home at a certain time. This interacted—unfavorably, as it turned out—with the second thing she realized, which was that she had failed to get an explicit commitment from him about when he would be home that evening. Instead, she had simply assumed he would be there when she expected and wanted him to be. She also discovered that she had ignored the fact that when he has been late it has always been for a good reason. Finally, she recognized Steve's work as a printer requires that once he starts a "run" he must see it through to the end, no matter how long it takes.

Using an example of your own when you felt an intense anger that you never want to feel again, consider the events leading up to and during your feeling of anger and identify if there was anything you did or did not do that contributed to your anger. For instance, were you maintaining realistic expectations? Did you unnecessarily take as personal whatever trespass was committed? Did you fail to take advantage of, or did you fail to create opportunities to be explicit about, your expectations?

Reviewing the events once again, what circumstances or actions of others contributed to your anger?

Jane knew that little could be done about the nature of Steve's work, so she decided upon a set of replacement behaviors that involved things that she could do to ensure that the occasion for her fury would not be created again. The first of these was to get an agreement from Steve to call her if he knew that he would be late getting home. (He had been assuming that because she knew the nature of his job there was no need for him to call.) In addition, Jane decided not to make any plans that included them both without first securing a commitment from Steve to be home at a certain time. And finally, when Steve was late getting home, Jane decided to remember to tell herself that "he'd be here if he could," for she knew that was true.

What replacement behaviors would keep your anger from happening again? Use the last two steps of the prevention format to make sure you can and will do them.

### *Inadequate*

Although no one at the party recognized it, Jim was in pain. On the outside, he smiled dutifully, made small talk when approached by others, and seemed particularly fond of strolling around the back yard by himself. On the inside, however, Jim was consumed by a feeling of inadequacy. Even his self-imposed exiles to the garden did little to take away the sting, for just being there was a demonstration of his inadequacy at being with others. As he stood there in the dark, cut off from his friends, Jim decided that he never wanted to feel this way again.

As Jim went through the prevention format, reviewing the events of that unpleasant evening, he realized that nothing had happened to him at the party to cause him to feel inadequate. The house was familiar to him, he was dressed appropriately, friends and strangers were warm and welcoming. He discovered that even before he arrived at the party, he had begun making pictures in his head of himself behaving and speaking awkwardly, and of people rejecting him as a result of his ineptness. He had been responding to these pictures, rather than to the actual people at the party. Accordingly, Jim began to catch himself making these images; and each time he did he changed them to portray a charming and responsive Jim who is respected and appreciated by others. The result was that rather than projecting and feeling inadequacy, he expressed confidence and well-being. Others responded well, of course, providing him with ample, undeniable demonstrations of his adequacy as a person.

You can probably recall a time when you felt painfully inadequate. Inadequacy requires your participation. Were you unfairly comparing yourself to others? (You have been playing tennis for only a year and yet you compared your skill to that of the top seeded players.) Did you use bad judgment in getting into the situation in the first place? (You have not yet graduated from high school, you have no jobs or skills to speak of, your girlfriend gets pregnant, and you decide to marry her.) Were the goals that you had set for yourself unrealistic? (You have just joined a large company as a junior executive and expect to become the company president within a couple of years.) Did you ignore your own strengths and attributes? (You are quailing at the thought of returning to school, having forgotten that you were a fine student in high school and college.)

Use the prevention format to provide yourself with the understandings, experiences, and behaviors that will allow you always to maintain feelings of adequacy. You deserve it.

## *What You Have Now*

When you were a kid you probably went through a period when you didn't want to go to bed because there were monsters in your closet. At the very least you needed enough light in the room to keep the monster locked securely away. For a while, bedtime was a dangerous time. As adults we still have our emotional monsters, but they have moved out of the closet and into the critical person who makes us feel ashamed, into the co-worker whose constant backstabbing arouses our anger, and into the friend who invariably humiliates us when he gets drunk.

You now have a way of dispelling those monsters, a format you can use to prevent the recurrence of emotional experiences that are, for you, thoroughly and unredeemably unpleasant. The Prevention format is appropriate when the benefits an emotion might offer are, to you, simply not worth the experiential toll the emotion exacts.

The Prevention format creates control in the service of protecting yourself. Having a way to protect yourself from very unpleasant emotions will create a sense of security, since those monsters will no longer be lurking in the world's closets, waiting to pounce upon your emotions. With understanding and control will come confidence in your ability to move securely through the world, and to explore the world more fully than you might otherwise have allowed yourself to.

What would the world be like if we were all able to prevent

ourselves from falling into the clutches of our emotional monsters? People would be happier, of course. More important, however, we would be more self-assured and confident, testing the various waters of the world with the knowledge that if our toes get nipped once it won't have to keep on happening. Knowing that, we can be more courageous about exploring our experience, and so discover things as individuals and as a world that might have otherwise been kept locked away from us.

# 12

# *Anticipation*

IT IS VERY LIKELY THAT YOU DON'T EARN YOUR BREAD AND butter in the same way your parents did. If you are a woman, you probably have worked outside of your home, and may even have a profession. It is also likely that you now live in a town or city far removed from the one in which you grew up. When elections roll around you probably vote. You have probably changed jobs at some point in your career, or perhaps you have gone back to school for an advanced degree, or to prepare yourself for a different profession. It's also likely that you have at least considered divorcing a spouse because you didn't get along. And you probably take all this freedom for granted.

Of course, there are places in the world today where such freedom to choose is unknown. Travel a few hundred years back in history and you will find that at that time there was *no* place where people knew the freedom to choose. In feudal Europe, for instance, if you were a male born to a father who was a coppersmith, you became a coppersmith. If your father was a nobleman, you became a nobleman. If he was a beggar, you begged. Surely, the beggar and the coppersmith dreamed of being noblemen, and perhaps the nobleman occasionally wished he could trade in his stuffed shirt for a leather apron, but no one took their musings seriously. They were dreams, nothing more, and everyone knew it. Women were in a similar but much smaller boat, since whether they were born to poverty or wealth, they were destined to have babies and manage households.

Look at how human beings have lived since societies were first organized thousands of years ago, and you will find that, for the most part, our billions of ancestors grew up, grew old, and died within a few miles of where they were born. It never occurred to them to do otherwise. They followed in the footsteps of their parents, living as they lived, working as they worked, believing as they believed. It never occurred to them to do otherwise. The laws of the land were in the hands of a very few. Everyone else was, essentially, a serf, not dedicated but *resigned* to acceding to the demands of their overlords. And again, it never occurred to them to do otherwise. Through the vast majority of human history, people's lives happened *to* them.

Then came America, with its Declaration of Independence, Bill of Rights, and Constitution, and the idea that individuals were responsible for their own destinies. Whether by accident, divine guidance, or human inspiration, somehow colonial America nurtured the notion that you were free to make of your life what you will. For the first time, personal control of one's destiny became a *societal* presupposition. Of course, this presupposition was not wholly fulfilled in reality—it took the 13th, 15th, and 19th amendments to the Constitution to make self-determination legal for minorities and women—and it has continued to be the case that there are people who find it easier to be serfs, or to "own" serfs, than to make choices. But now, at least, the idea is here, pervasive and indelible. Even if you decide to live and die where you were born, and work and believe just as your parents did, you can no longer take it for granted that you *had* to do those things. Now if you follow those footsteps, we do so because you choose to.

Now we take it for granted that we are free to choose our line of work or profession, free to generate whatever wealth we can, free to choose our spouses and free to leave them if the relationship proves unsatisfactory, free to live wherever we want to, free to decide who governs us and how, and so on. Few human beings in history have controlled their own destinies as strongly as we do right now, living in the United States. With television and motion pictures as our ambassadors, the idea of the right and ability to choose continues to spread throughout the world.

For the most part, however, that freedom to choose extends only to such external factors as employment, politics, mates, and so on. Most people still live in a feudal relationship to their emotions; emotions are something that just happen to them. Just as the coppersmith might have longed to be a banker, a jealous person now longs to feel trust, a bored person longs to feel excited, and a lonely person longs to feel connected. But these are longings. Dreams. They can fill our thoughts, but little can be done to turn those dreams into reality.

But the coppersmith was wrong. There is not and never was anything inherent in one man that made him fit to be a banker, while another was inherently fit only to be a coppersmith, or a beggar, or a barrister. Given the opportunity to learn, the mind of a coppersmith is as capable of grasping the difference between the left and right sides of a bank ledger, as the hands of a banker are capable of using a ball peen hammer to texture a copper tray. That the depth and range of your life are determined by the circumstances of your birth is, essentially, a genetic view, an *a priori* stance that, once accepted, automatically limits what you could even consider possible in terms of change.

The jealous, bored, and aloof dreamers who long to feel trust, excitement, and connection are wrong as well. In accepting the "genetic" orientation toward emotions they have also thrown up around themselves imaginary experiential fences. If these people were to but reach out and push against one of those fences they would see it dissolve. But the fences look real, and it seems that they have always been there. So it doesn't even occur to most people to test those fences; or if it does occur to them, they may not know how to go about it.

*The Emotional Hostage* is a guidebook, a manual for testing the mettle and merit of those emotional fences. We began our explorations by first recognizing that emotions have structure in terms of perceptions and thought processes (the "components"), and that structure has everything to do with creating and maintaining the emotions that you are feeling at a given moment. Our next step was to explore the components that make up the structure of emotions, discovering how the past, present, and future, sense of involvement, criteria, and so on, provide the warp and weft out of which our emotional experiences are woven.

But having choice about your emotions means more than merely being able to shift from one feeling to another. Shifts in emotion should be worth taking, and be appropriate for the situation you are in or the outcome you desire. And so we considered the relationship between emotions and the contexts in which they occur. We found that there is an appropriateness of emotional experience that is not absolute, but is relative to who you are, to your needs, and to the context you are in. With that idea under our belts, we were ready to tackle the appropriate selection of emotions for new contexts (Before), for ongoing contexts (During), and for recurring contexts (After).

Of course, the greatest choice in the world is no more than a happy thought, unless it is somehow put into effect. So we turned to exploring various means of accessing emotions, including *tapping your emotions*, *self-anchoring*, and *breaking cause-effects*. Also among these techniques was that of *remodeling*, which is close to the heart of emotional choice because of its direct use of the fact that our emotions are the simultaneous experiencing of certain sets of components.

Still, it's one thing to speak, and another to be understood. Your emotions are a fundamental and pervasive aspect of who you are as a person; the only way that others can know who you are and what is going on within you is through your expressive behavior. And so we explored emotional expression, which is the link between you and the rest of the world.

We then moved on to the darker realm of monstrous emotions, those over which we seem to have no control, and learned how to declaw, defang, and, if necessary, avoid them.

Now you do know how. You may not be facile yet with the concepts, distinctions, and formats, but these are relatively low hurdles that, with a little thought and dedicated practice, will soon be behind you. The highest hurdle of them all is already behind you. If you look back you may still get a glimpse of it. It was the one that said, Emotions are something that happen *to* you. What you have to look forward to is the joy of feeling what you want to feel, the fulfillment of being congruent, the satisfaction of expressing yourself in a way that is understood by others, and the freedom to determine your own emotional destiny.

You will be able to reach out and, with a touch, dissolve your own emotional fences. There are, however, still all of those emotional coppersmiths, bankers, and beggars out there, wishing for more, but trying to cope with what they've got. We believe completely, however, that if everyone enjoyed the ongoing experience of emotional choice, the level of widespread accurate communication and personal emotional satisfaction would usher in an era of understanding, tolerance, and cooperation that would, by comparison, dwarf any previous age of peaceful and enlightened coexistence. So much of our energies are devoted to coping with our unpleasant or inappropriate feelings and wrestling with the misleading emotional expressions of others that, once relieved of those burdens, we would as a species be freer to turn our congruent and cooperative attentions to making the present and future more nearly what we would like them to be. Toward the fulfillment of that outcome, we hope and trust that the ideas and personal technologies presented in this book will not be forgotten on a dusty shelf, but will find their way into the hands of every coppersmith who looks in the mirror and sees a banker smiling back at him.

# *The Formats at a Glance*

## *Chapter 3: Emotions Are the Source*

*Emotions are our global subjective responses at a given moment.*

*Emotions are distinct from part-body feelings that may be going on at the same time.*

*Emotions are distinct from the behaviors they help generate.*

*Emotions are distinct from the value judgments we make about them.*

THE FOUR KEY ABILITIES OF EMOTIONAL CHOICE

| | |
|---|---|
| *Placement* | The ability to respond to life's situations with emotions that are appropriate and useful |
| *Expression* | The ability to choose how to express emotions |
| *Employment* | The ability to utilize unpleasant emotions to generate useful behaviors and pleasant emotions |
| *Prevention* | The ability to prevent yourself from experiencing certain overwhelming and immobilizing emotions |

## *Chapter 4: The Structure of Emotions*

*Emotions Have Structure*

*Knowing Structure Leads to Appropriateness*

*Knowing Structure Allows You to Change Your Emotions*

*Knowing Structure Gives You Access to All Emotions*

## *Chapter 5: The Pieces of the Puzzle*

**The Components of Emotions**

*Time Frame*
*Modality*
*Involvement*
*Intensity*
*Comparison*
*Tempo*
*Criteria*
*Chunk Size*

## *Chapter 6: Orienting to Your Emotions*

*Placement* ⟶ *Orient* *Select* *Access*
*Expression*
*Employment*
*Prevention*

*Format for orienting to emotions:*

1. Identify a familiar situation. Imagine yourself in that situation, clearly and in detail. What do you see? What do you hear?
2. When you have firmly established the scene, select an emotion. Imagine feeling that emotion in that familiar situation to discover what your response would be. You can use the following question for your explorations:

   If I feel ______*(emotion)*______ in this situation, what will be the consequences?
3. When you have thoroughly explored your reaction, select another emotion and imagine feeling it in the same context. Notice how your reaction to the situation changes in response to the new emotion.
4. Holding the situation constant, run through as many emotions as you wish, observing the variations in your response.

## *Chapter 7: Selecting Your Emotions*

*"After" Selection Format:*

1. Identify an experience you had with which you are now dissatisfied because of your feelings and/or your behavior at the time; then evaluate what happened in terms of "What was going on?" and "What did I want?" (The answers to these questions could include emotions, behaviors, or outcomes.)
2. Determine how you would have liked to behave.
3. Now make your best guess at what emotion you would need to feel in order to generate that behavior.
4. Once you find an emotion that you think would have helped you behave as you would have liked, imagine that same kind of situation occurring in the future and, holding constant the emotion you have selected, imagine how it will affect your experience and behavior. Be sure to include in your consideration the responses of others, the preservation of your own well-being, and effectiveness in achieving your desired outcomes. If the emotion you have selected seems inappropriate or insufficient, then cycle back to step 3 and either choose a different emotion or add another to the one you have already selected.

5. If the emotion you have selected fulfills your desired outcome for that particular situation, be sure you have access to it so that you can feel the way you want to feel the next time you find yourself in that situation.

### *"During" Selection Format:*

1. When you become aware that your current experience is somehow unsatisfactory, specify just how you are feeling and behaving in this situation.
2. Take a deep breath, then "step away from yourself." (In your imagination, see yourself in the situation, thus becoming a detached spectator for the moment.) From this detached perspective, ask yourself, "What do I want? What is my desired outcome?"
3. Select one or more feelings that would be more useful in getting what you want in the current situation.
4. Identify what behaviors are the *natural consequences* of the emotion that you want to feel in this situation. That is, what are the behaviors that you naturally engage in when feeling that emotion? Are these behaviors ones that will work to your benefit in getting what you want? If the answer is no, then cycle back to step 3 and choose a different emotion you might want to have in this situation.
5. Imagine feeling the emotion that you have selected, and consider how events are likely to proceed with you feeling that way. Be sure to include in your consideration the responses of others, the preservation of your own well-being, and your effectiveness in achieving your desired outcomes. If the emotion you have selected is not enough to satisfy your needs, cycle back to step 3 and add any other emotions that you think will be appropriate.
6. Shift to a means of accessing the emotion(s) you want to have in the ongoing situation.

### *"Before" Selection Format:*

1. Describe the situation, specifically including what about it is familiar and what about it is new and unfamiliar to you.
2. Consider what you want to accomplish in this situation, even if it is only to enjoy yourself, or to be helpful, or to protect yourself.

3. Decide what you want to feel in this situation.
4. Identify what behaviors are natural consequences of the emotion that you would like to feel in this situation. That is, what are the behaviors that you naturally engage in when feeling that emotion?

   Are these behaviors ones you want in the upcoming situation? Are they compatible with the outcomes that you have set for the situation? If the answer is no, then cycle back to step 3 and choose a different emotion you might want to have in this situation.
5. Imagine being in the upcoming situation, feeling the emotion that you have selected, and evaluate how events are likely to proceed. Be sure to include in your evaluation the responses of others, the preservation of your own well-being, and your effectiveness in achieving your desired outcomes. If the emotion you have selected is not enough to satisfy your needs, cycle back to step 3 and add any other emotions that you think will be appropriate.
6. Shift to a means of accessing the emotion(s) you want to have in the upcoming situation.

## *Chapter 8: Accessing Your Emotions*

The four methods for accessing emotions are *tapping emotions*, *self-anchoring*, *breaking cause-effects*, and *remodeling*.

You can "tap" an emotion using:

*A Memory*
*A Fantasy*
*Adjusting Your Body*
*Redirecting Attention*
*Changing Time Frame*
*Changing Intensity*
*Changing Tempo*
*Changing Involvement*
*Changing Criteria*
*Changing Chunk Size*
*Looking For What Is Missing or What Is There*

*Format for Tapping Your Emotions:*

1. Specify how you want to feel. This information may come from the results of one of the "selection" formats.
2. Ask yourself, "What could I do here and now (or there and then) to get to that emotion?"
3. By searching through your personal history, identify ways that have worked before for you or an acquaintance to access the emotion you have selected.
4. Select the means that seems most appropriate.
5. Do it. If the result is not satisfying, cycle back through steps 3 and 4 and select another means of accessing the emotion.

*Format for Self-Anchoring:*

1. Identify the feeling you want to have.
2. Remember a time when you experienced that emotion fully. When you have identified the memory, clasp your hands together lightly (or use any other discreet touch signal, such as holding your earlobe between your thumb and forefinger, or touching the side of your nose).
3. Step back into that memory, seeing what you saw, hearing what you heard, and, most important, feeling what you felt then.
4. Once you have immersed yourself in the desired emotion, gently increase the pressure of your clasp or touch as you continue feeling the emotion fully. This action establishes the clasping of your hands, or other touch signal, as the anchor for the feeling.
5. Maintaining the pressure of your touch, reorient yourself to your present surroundings, bringing the emotion with you. If, upon reorienting yourself to the present, the emotion subsides, go back through steps 3 and 4 and reaccess the memory and reanchor.
6. Release your hands and enjoy how you feel. If the feeling subsides, perform your touch signal again to reaccess the emotion. Do this until you can both access the emotion using your anchor, and maintain it for a while after you release the anchor.
7. Later, test your anchor by once again pressing your hands together, or touching in the particular way you have decided on. If the anchor does not access the desired emotion, go back through the technique, being sure to intensify the memory as strongly as possible, and adding other memories if necessary.

### *Format for Breaking Cause-Effects:*

1. Identify what is making you feel an emotion that is unpleasant or inappropriate (that is, identify the cause).
2. Select a way to nullify the effect of that cause by either (a) Changing your perspective to that of being in the future looking back, or to that of being an outside observer, or (b) Shifting your attention to another stimulus, or (c) Physically removing yourself.
3. Remove yourself in the way that you have selected. If you still feel overwhelmed, go back to step 2 and select another, perhaps more dramatic way to nullify the cause-effect.
4. If you wish, once you have nullified the effect of the stimulus you can move to the During format and to other accessing approaches.

### *Exercise for Experimenting with the Remodeling of Emotions:*

1. Identify an emotion that you are experiencing.
2. Identify the significant components of the emotion by asking yourself, "How do I know I'm feeling ___*(the emotion)*___ as compared to any other emotion?"

   That is, as you consider the time frame, tempo, modality, degree of involvement, intensity, matching/mismatching/comparing, criteria, and chunk size, what seems to stand out as significant in making that emotion what it is?
3. Change one of the significant components in some qualitative or quantitative way.
4. Notice how your emotions change as a result of the changes you make in the components of your experience.

### *Format for Remodeling Emotions:*

1. Become aware of the significant components underlying an unwanted emotion.
2. Change the qualities of those components, one at a time.
3. Evaluate whether that change leads you toward attaining the emotion you want to have.
4. Continue to change significant components of the unwanted emotion until you have attained the emotion you desire.

## Chapter 9: Expressing Your Emotions

### *Expression Format:*

1. Identify the emotion that you have been expressing in a way that is unsatisfactory to you.
2. Identify what you want to accomplish through your expression of this emotion.
3. Generate at least five possible expressions of this emotion. In doing this you can use your own past experiences and examples of other people's behavior, as well as creating new possibilities.
4. For each possibility, run a "movie" in which you see yourself feeling the emotion and expressing it in that way. Decide which possible expression(s) appears most useful, given what you want to accomplish. If none of the possibilities appears useful and appropriate, then cycle back to the previous step and generate other possibilities.
5. With the expression(s) you have selected, replay the movie, this time refining your behavior further and checking to make sure that it will indeed lead to the outcomes you desire for that situation.
6. Step into the movie, *feel* the emotion, and imagine as fully as possible how it will be to express it in this way.
7. Identify an upcoming situation in which you are likely to experience the emotion. Imagine being in that situation, feeling the emotion, and expressing it in the way you have chosen.
8. Repeat step 7 for at least two other upcoming situations, making minor adjustments in your behavior if necessary. If you discover that there are certain contexts for which your new form of expression is inappropriate, run through the sequence again, beginning with step 2, for that different context.

## Chapter 10: Employing Your Emotions

The essential pattern that underlies all generative chains:

*Triggering emotion*
↳ *Respect/appreciation*
↳ *Curiosity*
↳ *Reassurance*
↳ *Confidence*

## *Generative Chain for "Regret"*

1. Recognize that you are feeling regretful.
2. Feel respectful and appreciative toward your feeling of regret as being a signal that you need to do something to ensure that you don't repeat the same mistake in the future.
3. With a feeling of curiosity, evaluate your mistake with respect to what you could have done to avoid making it.
4. Recall memories of mistakes you have made (past sources of regrets) that you corrected once you knew what to do. Use these examples as a basis for feeling reassured.
5. Imagine a future situation in which you do what you have identified should have been done in the situation you feel regretful about. Make this rich and vivid rehearsal of the future compelling enough that it fills you with confidence about your ability to actually fulfill that future.

## *Generative Chain for "Frustration"*

1. Recognize that you are feeling frustrated in a particular situation.
2. Feel respectful and appreciative toward your feeling of frustration as being a signal that you need to do something different, in terms of learning, changing your perspective, readjusting your expectations, or varying your behavior.
3. With a feeling of curiosity, evaluate whether the outcome is still worth going after. If it's not, then drop the outcome and go on to other pursuits. If it is, continue on with the next step.
4. Search through your past for experiences in which you overcame similar difficulties by changing your approach. Feel reassured by the fact that you have successfully overcome obstacles.
5. Imagine yourself in the future, responding to situations that you find frustrating by changing your approach, and then attaining your outcome, feeling confident about your ability to do that.

## *Generative Chain for "Anxiety"*

1. Recognize that you are feeling anxious.

2. Remember that feeling anxious is a signal to you that there is something in your future for which you need to better prepare, and feel respect and appreciation for that emotion as a vital signal.
3. With a feeling of curiosity, evaluate what you need to do to better prepare. This may involve gathering information to fill in your picture of the future, marshalling or acquiring certain skills, or establishing a positively stated outcome.
4. Recall examples from your past when you have done what you now need to do to meet this future challenge or threat, feeling reassured as you recall these memories of your capability.
5. Imagine yourself in the future preparing to meet the future challenge or threat, repeating this rehearsal until you feel confident about your ability to do what you need to do.

### *Generative Chain for "Hopelessness"*

1. Recognize that you are feeling hopeless.
2. Feel respectful and appreciative toward your feeling of hopelessness as a signal that it's time to let go of some outcome that you have been unsuccessfully striving to attain.
3. With a feeling of curiosity, evaluate whether there is anything else that you can reasonably do. If your answer is yes, then go to feeling frustrated as a first step to feeling challenged and determined, and to generating alternative ways to try to get what you want. If the answer is no, go on to the next step.
4. Recall examples from your past of times when you let go of certain outcomes, large or small, and thereby freed yourself to turn to other things. Find enough examples so that you feel reassured about your ability to do this.
5. Imagine yourself in the future, walking away from outcomes that you simply can't attain, feeling confident about your ability to do that.

### *Generative Chain for "Stuck"*

1. Recognize that you feel stuck.
2. Recognize that you need to generate other options for yourself in this situation, and feel respectful and appreciative toward the important emotional signal you have given yourself.

3. With a feeling of curiosity, evaluate the approaches to which you have been confining yourself in trying to attain your outcome.
4. Recall times when you have been stuck and have changed how you were thinking about the situation so that you were able to generate another way to go; feel reassured about your ability to do this.
5. Go into the future, imagining yourself feeling stuck and then generating new options that make it possible for you to keep moving forward. Repeat and make these futures increasingly vivid until you feel confident about your ability to generate new options when you feel stuck.

## *Generative Chain for "Anger"*

1. Recognize that you are feeling angry.
2. Feel respectful and appreciative toward your feeling of anger as an important signal letting you know that someone (possibly yourself) has violated an important standard of yours.
3. With a feeling of curiosity, evaluate what you can do in the future to prevent your standard from being similarly violated, and how you could more usefully respond when your standard is violated despite your efforts to prevent it. If you don't know what to do, gather information from people who seem to be able to respond usefully to such angering situations.
4. Recall past times when you have prevented or usefully responded to the violation of your standards, and feel reassured about your ability to do it.
5. (a) Imagine the next time your standard might be violated and see yourself doing something to prevent it from happening. Rerun this future until you feel confident about your ability to respond in the way that you would like to.

   (b) It may be that, despite your best efforts, you can't prevent others from violating your standards. You should therefore also imagine your standards being violated anyway and how you could respond more usefully. (You may need to turn to the formats in the contextualizing and accessing chapters to help you with this step.) Again, rerun this future until you feel confident that you will be able to respond in a satisfying and effective way.

### *Generative Chain for "Guilt"*

1. Recognize that you are feeling guilty in a particular situation.
2. With respect and appreciation, recognize that your feeling guilty is a signal that you have violated a personal standard and that you need to make sure that you do not do it again in the future.
3. With a feeling of curiosity, evaluate whether the standard you have violated is one that is worth maintaining. If it is not worth maintaining, then you can update, replace, or discard it.
4. Recall personal experiences in which you lived up to your personal standards, even though it was difficult to do. As you accumulate these examples, feel reassured about your ability to live up to your personal standards.
5. Imagine living up to your standards in upcoming situations that will severely test you, and feel confident about your ability to do so.

### *Generative Chain for "Disappointment"*

1. Recognize that you feel disappointed.
2. With respect and appreciation, recognize that your feeling of disappointment is a signal that you need to reevaluate your outcomes.
3. With a feeling of curiosity, evaluate whether what you wanted and did not get is worth continuing to want. If it is, then go to step 4a. If what you wanted and did not get is no longer worth wanting, consider what would be more worthwhile to want under the circumstances, then go to step 4b.
4. (a) If what you wanted is still worth pursuing, recall memories of persevering and eventually finding ways to get what you wanted, and feel reassured about your ability to do that.

   (b) If it is time to find other things to pursue, recall times when you changed goals and eventually succeeded at getting what you wanted, and feel reassured about your ability to do that.
5. Imagine doing what you need to do to eventually get what you want, adding detail and vividness until you feel confident about that future.

### *Generative Chain for "Loneliness"*

1. Recognize that you are feeling lonely.

2. With respect and appreciation, recognize your feeling as a signal of your need for a particular kind of contact or connection with someone.
3. With a feeling of curiosity, evaluate what kind of contact you want and with whom.
4. Search through your memories to find examples of times when *you* initiated such contact, and feel reassured about your ability to make contact with others.
5. Step into the future and imagine yourself initiating the kind of contact you want to have with the people you have chosen, increasing the vividness of your pictures until you feel confident about your future ability.

### *Generative Chain for "Jealousy"*

1. Recognize that you are feeling jealous.
2. With respect and appreciation for the signal value of feeling jealous, recognize that your jealousy is a signal that you need to take care of your emotional well-being.
3. With a feeling of curiosity, evaluate whether your well-being actually is in jeopardy. If it's not, then move to enjoying the fact that your loved one is having a good time with others. If it is, proceed with steps 4 and 5.
4. Recall times in your past when you have taken care of yourself, finding enough examples so that you feel reassured about your ability to do what you need to in order to maintain your well-being.
5. Looking to the future, imagine yourself successfully taking care of yourself in situations in which there really is a threat to your well-being. Be sure that these futures are vivid enough to make you feel confident.

## *Chapter 11: Prevention*

### *Prevention Format:*

1. Identify the emotion you are feeling, making sure that it is one that you are unwilling to experience again in the situation in which you felt it.

2. By running a movie in your head of the events leading up to and during the time you felt that emotion, identify what, if anything, you did to contribute to its occurrence. Look at your behavior from at least two points of view—your own and someone else's.

3. Rerunning that internal movie of what happened, identify what, if any, external causes (circumstances, other people's behavior, etc.) contributed to your experiencing the unwanted emotion.

4. Combining your findings from the previous two steps, come up with replacement behaviors (corrections) that would make it impossible for you to experience that unwanted emotion again in that situation.

5. Make sure that you *can* do those replacement behaviors by searching your personal history for examples of your having done them, even if in other types of situations. You may also be able to assure yourself that you can do the replacement behaviors by recalling having seen others do them—examples that you *know* you could do as well. If you can't find either personal or vicarious examples of the replacement behaviors you will need, then go back to step 4 and come up with other, simpler or more familiar behaviors. (If the behaviors you need are not within your present experience and are irreplaceable for getting the outcome you want, then you will need to learn them before you will be able to avoid a recurrence of the emotion-triggering situation.) As a check for yourself, consider the question, How do you know you *can* do the replacement behaviors you will need?

6. Now, *will* you do those replacement behaviors? Is your commitment strong enough? Create a movie in which you see yourself successfully doing the needed behaviors.

7. Next, rerun that movie, this time from the perspective of being *within* it, seeing what you would see through your own eyes if you were actually there, hearing what you would hear, and feeling what you would feel. Make sure that your movie is vivid and rich in detail. As a check for yourself, consider the question, How do you know you *will* do these behaviors? (Remember that you are not figuring out what to do once you are in, and want to get out of, that unwanted emotion, but what to do to prevent your getting into that emotion in the first place.)

# References

Cameron-Bandler, Leslie. *Solutions: Practical and Effective Antidotes for Sexual and Relationship Problems*. San Rafael, CA: FuturePace, 1985.

Cameron-Bandler, Leslie; Gordon, David; and Lebeau, Michael. *Know How: Guided Programs for Inventing Your Own Best Future*. San Rafael, CA: FuturePace, 1985.

Cameron-Bandler, Leslie; Gordon, David; and Lebeau, Michael. *The* EMPRINT *Method: A Guide to Reproducing Competence*. San Rafael, CA: FuturePace, 1985.

Cousins, Norman. *Anatomy of an Illness*. New York: Bantam Books, 1980.

__________. *The Healing Heart*. New York: W.W. Norton & Co., 1983.

Darwin, Charles. *The Expression of the Emotions in Man and Animals*. Chicago, IL: The University of Chicago Press, 1965.

Eliot, Robert S. and Breo, Dennis L. *Is It Worth Dying For?* New York: Bantam Books, 1984.

Enright, John. *Therapy Without Resistance*. Tiburon, CA: Enright Press, 1980.

Gould, Stephen Jay. *The Mismeasure of Man*. New York: W.W. Norton & Co., 1981.

Hall, Edward T. *The Silent Language*. Garden City, NY: Doubleday & Co., 1959.

________. *The Hidden Dimension*. Garden City, NY: Doubleday & Co., 1966.

________. *Beyond Culture*. Garden City, NY: Anchor Press/ Doubleday, 1976.

________. *The Dance of Life*. Garden City, NY: Anchor Press/ Doubleday, 1983.

Hofstadter, Douglas R. *Godel, Escher, Bach: An Eternal Golden Braid*. New York: Vintage Books, 1979.

Kuhn, Thomas S. *The Structure of Scientific Revolutions*. Chicago, IL: The University of Chicago Press, 1970.

Lynch, James J. *The Language of the Heart*. New York: Basic Books, 1985.

Mandler, G. *Mind and Emotion*. Melbourne, FL: Kreiger, 1982.

Miller, George A.; Galanter, Eugene; and Pribram, Karl. *Plans and the Structure of Behavior*. New York: Holt, Rinehart and Winston, 1960.

Newell, Allen and Simon, Herbert A. *Human Problem Solving*. Englewood Cliffs, NJ: Prentice-Hall, 1972.

Ornstein, Robert E. *The Psychology of Consciousness*. New York: Harcourt Brace Jovanovich, 1977.

Plutchik, R. and Kellerman, H., eds. *Theories of Emotion*, vol. 1 of *Emotion: Theory, Research, and Experience*. New York: Academic Press, 1980.

Polya, George. *Patterns of Plausible Inference*. Princeton, NJ: Princeton University Press, 1954.

Pribram, Karl. *Languages of the Brain*. Englewood Cliffs, NJ: Prentice-Hall, 1971.

Watzlawick, Paul; Beavin, Janet Helmick; and Jackson, Don D. *Pragmatics of Human Communication*. New York: W.W. Norton & Co., 1967.

*Dear Reader,*

We would like to send you a gift.

Now that you have learned so much about responding to and changing your own emotions, it's time to turn your attention to the emotions of your family, friends, and associates. We have developed two formats that will teach you how to recognize and influence the emotional states of others.

If you would like a free copy of these valuable techniques, we would be delighted to send them to you as a way of expressing our thanks for your interest in this book.

Send us your name and address and we will mail them to you at no charge:

MICHAEL LEBEAU AND LESLIE CAMERON-BANDLER

c/o FuturePace, Inc.
P.O. Box 1173
San Rafael, CA 94915